THE SMOKING BACON & HOG COOKBOOK

THE **SMOKING**

BACON

BILL GILLESPIE

PIT MASTER OF SMOKIN' HOGGZ BBQ,
ONE OF THE MOST DECORATED TEAMS
IN THE COUNTRY

WITH **TIM O'KEEFE**

& HOG

COOKBOOK

THE WHOLE PIG &
NOTHING BUT THE PIG BBQ RECIPES

PAGE STREET
PUBLISHING CO.

PAGE STREET
PUBLISHING CO.

First published in 2016 by

Page Street Publishing Co.

27 Congress Street, Suite 103

Salem, MA 01970

www.pagestreetpublishing.com

Distributed by Macmillan, sales in Canada by The Canadian Manda Group.

19   18   17   16   1   2   3   4   5

ISBN-13: 978-1-62414-224-6

ISBN-10: 1-62414-224-9

Library of Congress Control Number: 2015952077

Cover and book design by Page Street Publishing Co.

Photography by Ken Goodman

Printed and bound in China

Page Street is proud to be a member of 1% for the Planet. Members donate one percent of their sales to one or more of the over 1,500 environmental and sustainability charities across the globe who participate in this program.

THIS BOOK IS DEDICATED TO MY MOTHER, DIANE
GILLESPIE, WHO FROM DAY ONE HAS ALWAYS BELIEVED
IN ME AND ENCOURAGED ME TO FOLLOW MY DREAMS.
YOU ARE THE MOST LOVING AND CARING WOMAN I
HAVE EVER KNOWN. I LOVE YOU, MOM!

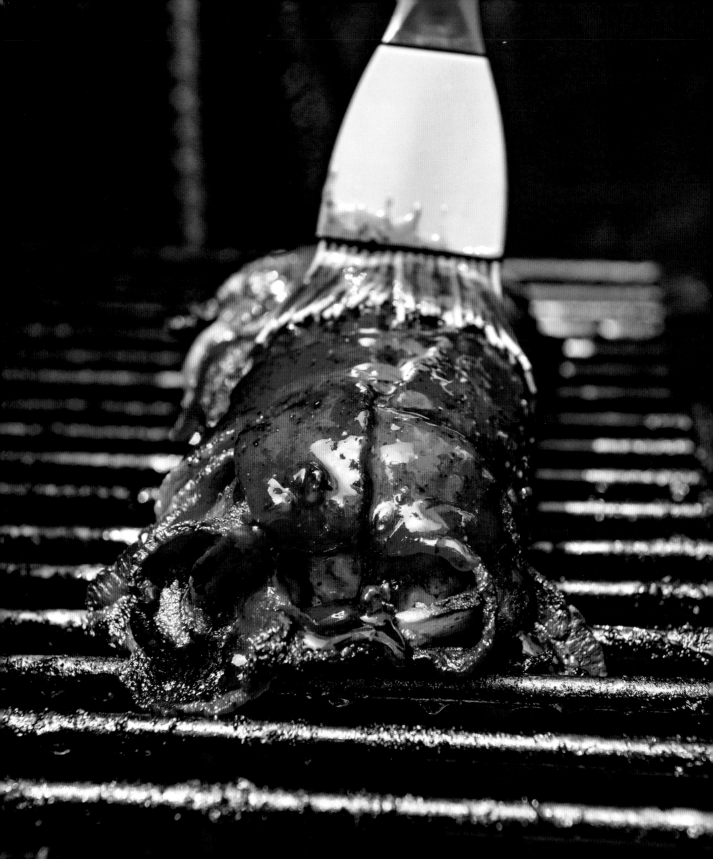

CONTENTS

CHAPTER 1

THE PIG, THE WHOLE PIG AND NOTHING BUT THE PIG

When I first got involved in competition barbecue back in 2005, I never could have imagined all the things that would happen to me. Competition barbecue is unlike anything else I've ever experienced. Sure, each event is a competition to see who the best is that day, but the barbecue community is truly a community of friendship. Along the way, I've made several friends with whom I've shared a lot of laughs, and for that alone, I'll always be thankful.

Since 2008, my competition team, Smokin' Hoggz, has won several trophies, including the Jack Daniel's World Championship Invitational Barbecue in 2011 and the American Royal Invitational in 2014, arguably the two most prestigious titles in competition barbecue. When I cooked at these contests, I used the same types of smokers I discuss in this cookbook. At the Jack, I cooked on an insulated cabinet-style smoker and a non-insulated bullet-style smoker. At the Royal, I cooked exclusively on an insulated cabinet smoker. Success on the competition circuit led to new opportunities, such as writing the barbecue cookbook *Secrets to Smoking*, and bringing a commercial barbecue sauce to market—things I never would have imagined were possible.

When the Smokin' Hoggz team competes at barbecue contests, we're required to submit four entries: chicken, pork ribs, pork shoulder and beef brisket. Given that two of the four categories are pork, I've had a lot of practice cooking swine. Additionally, one of my favorite foods is bacon. The book you are reading actually came out of an idea I had to create a bacon cookbook—that's why nearly a third of the recipes use bacon.

Over the years on the competition circuit, I have had lots of people ask me questions about pork. Some people wanted to learn how to cook pork, while others asked about the difference between pork butt and picnic shoulder. Eventually, I decided to combine my interest in teaching people about pork with my love for bacon, and created the book you're holding in your hands.

Secrets to Smoking focused on techniques and recipes for making award-winning barbecue. This book is a little different. Although it uses many of the same cooking techniques, the main focus is on showing the versatility of the pig by teaching people how to use different parts of the animal to create tasty dishes.

HOGS, PIGS AND SWINE

Like a lot of people, I pretty much used the terms *hog, pig and swine* interchangeably. I wasn't sure whether these words really meant the same thing or were somehow different. So, I did what a lot of guys my age might do. I opened up an old, dusty dictionary to see what it had to say. In one source, pig was described as a young, domestic swine that is not yet sexually mature; however, the term can also be used more broadly to simply mean a wild or domestic hog. Although hog is a synonym for pig, it can technically mean a male pig that has had its sex organs removed (and you thought the pig ending up on the smoker was the worst thing that could ever happen to it). Swine was described as a short-legged mammal with thick, bristly skin and a long, flexible snout. I'm still not sure how rigid these distinctions are, so I guess the important thing for you to understand is that I use these words interchangeably in this book. After all, I don't breed hogs; I cook 'em.

There are several types of hogs that animal breeders might raise. On the following pages are some descriptions of the ones most frequently found on smokers. These are all heritage breeds, which are more expensive than commodity pork found at most grocery stores. Small butcher shops might carry heritage breeds, but your best bet to locate some might be through a dedicated breeder or specialty farm in your area.

I like Hampshire, Berkshire and duroc for shoulders, butts and ribs. I particularly like Berkshire because I think it produces a richer pork flavor, and I frequently use this breed in barbecue competitions.

YORKSHIRE
Yorkshires are a rather lean and muscular breed with a smaller quantity of back fat. These large, white hogs have upward-pointing, triangular ears and short snouts. They're known for raising large litters and are the most popular breed in the United States.

BERKSHIRE (KUROBUTA)
This dark-colored breed is highly renowned for superior meat quality. Chances are the meat from a Berkshire hog has better color, texture and marbling than any other swine you're likely to find on a smoker. They are prized for long, slow cooks.

DUROC
The duroc is a breed of red hog that is known for its ability to grow quickly and easily, acquiring more meat in the meantime. Many mixed-breed, commercial pigs trace their ancestors to duroc hogs. Their numbers in the United States are second only to Yorkshires.

HAMPSHIRE
Some people believe the Hampshire is the oldest breed of hog in the United States. Well muscled, these hogs produce a higher ratio of lean meat than do most other breeds. They are characterized by a black complexion with a swath of white that spans the front shoulders and legs.

HEREFORD
Herefords are known for their brown-and-white color, similar to cattle. This breed originated in the United States and is popular in the Midwest. These hardy animals can grow to 700–800 pounds (318–363 kg).

TAMWORTH

Red hogs that originated in Britain, Tamworths sport a long, narrow body that is reputable for developing quality hams. These hogs grow slowly and spend lots of time outdoors foraging for food.

LARGE BLACK

Native to England, this is the only hog in the United States that is all black. These long animals can be found in pastures. They're docile animals that provide very large litters, with huge, floppy ears that partially cover their faces.

TYPES OF SMOKERS

Cooking on a smoker is absolutely my favorite way to make pork. One obvious reason is that the smoke helps create a unique flavor. Another is the resulting texture of the meat. When you cook using a smoker, you're cooking over a low temperature for a long time period. Slow cooking allows the fibers and tough tissues that make up muscle regions to break down. Similarly, this cooking method will melt down some of the fat surrounding the muscle, adding moisture and flavor to the meat.

There are a wide variety of styles of smokers on the market. Some people prefer to actually build their own cooking device. Although most people on the competition circuit prefer to purchase a smoker, every once in a while I find someone who has built one. The three main types of smokers most frequently used are offset barrel smokers, non-insulated bullet-style smokers and insulated cabinet smokers.

NON-INSULATED BULLET-STYLE SMOKERS

Non-insulated smokers, such as the Weber Smokey Mountain Cooker (WSM), are sometimes referred to as bullet smokers because of their shape. Although they are not insulated, they tend to have a slow burn rate and do a pretty good job of maintaining a constant temperature. All the recipes in this book can be made using a non-insulated smoker. With a low price point of $300 or $400, these smokers are a great purchase for backyard cooking enthusiasts. I know a lot of people on the competition circuit who have used these products with excellent results!

INSULATED CABINET SMOKERS

In my opinion, insulated cabinet smokers, such as my Humphrey's smoker, are top-of-the-line products. These smokers cost anywhere from $500 up to around $9,000. I like insulated cabinet smokers because I think they provide more consistent heat, especially during cold weather, with little fluctuation in temperature during the cooking process.

A cabinet-style smoker cooks food using a reverse-flow effect. These smokers have an interior wall that runs parallel to the exterior walls that make up the sides of the smoker. Heat and smoke travel up between the interior and exterior walls of the smoker, and then back down from the top of the smoker toward the cooking chamber. In the cooking chamber, air flows over the meat, cooking and flavoring the food, and then exits the bottom of the smoker. I like to cook picnic shoulder and brisket with the fat cap facing up to protect the meat from the direct flow of heat and smoke. During the cooking process, the fat cap renders down, which helps keep the meat moist and juicy—self-basting, you could say. All of the recipes in this book can be cooked using an insulated cabinet smoker.

OFFSET BARREL SMOKERS

Offset barrel smokers are what many people first think of when they think of a smoker. Typically, the fire is created in a small box offset from a separate compartment with a much larger cooking area. The smoke and heat travel from the firebox and slowly fill up the cooking area, cooking the food in the process. The fire for these smokers can require a lot of work, particularly during longer cooking sessions. None of the recipes in this book are cooked using an offset smoker, but all of them can easily be adapted to this type of smoker.

I'm a competition barbecue cook. Offset barrel smokers are not my preferred style of smoker because tending the fire for a long duration can be a chore. I prefer not to have this additional task during a competition, but if you think maintaining the fire is part of the fun, then a barrel smoker is a great option for your backyard! You can purchase an entry model for around $200, while a competition-worthy rig can run as much as $10,000.

WATER PANS: Non-insulated smokers and insulated cabinet smokers have water pans. The water pan acts as a heat sink, which helps the overall cooking temperature stabilize. The water also contributes a bit of moisture, which helps prevent the meat from drying out during the cooking process. Some of the recipes in this book use a water pan, while others do not. If you do not use a water pan when you cook, the temperature of the cooker will run a little bit higher. If your cooker doesn't have a water pan and you want to use one, you can use a disposable aluminum pan filled halfway with water.

SMOKE WOODS, CHIPS AND CHUNKS

In traditional barbecue, a primary component of the basic flavor profile is wood smoke. In essence, wood smoke is just another ingredient that adds flavor to meat. If you use too much smoke, the food can taste bitter. If you use too little smoke, the flavor of the food may be missing just a little something and fall flat. In addition to learning how much wood smoke to use while cooking, you'll need to learn how to pair different types of wood with various meats and seafood. Don't worry, though: I won't make you learn it all on your own. This section should provide a great foundation to help you get started.

Smoke woods generally break down into two main groups: nut woods and fruit woods. In general, we think nut wood pairs better with beef, and fruit wood pairs better with pork and poultry. The following table provides descriptions of different smoke woods frequently used on the competition barbecue circuit.

WOOD TYPE	DESCRIPTION
Alder	Alder, a mild wood from the Pacific Northwest, is good to use with seafood, poultry, pork and light game.
Hickory	Hickory is a popular wood that lends a hint of bacon flavor to the food you are cooking, and goes well with both pork and beef.
Mesquite	Mesquite is typically associated with Texas barbecue, and works well with beef. Use a little at first to get adjusted to the flavor, as mesquite can easily dominate the flavor of your food.
Pecan	Pecan is an all-around good wood for smoking. It has a sweet and mild flavor that is similar to that of hickory.
Sugar Maple	Frequently found in the Northeast and a staple on the competition scene, sugar maple provides a mellow smoke flavor. Try mixing one or two pieces of this wood with apple or cherry for some interesting flavor combinations. It works well with poultry, pork and cheese.
Walnut	Walnut produces a heavy flavor that lends itself well to beef more so than pork or poultry. I think walnut is best when used alone. If you want to mix flavors, try adding some fruit wood.
Apple	Perhaps the most common of the fruit woods, apple lends itself well to pork and chicken. Apple provides a mild, subtle fruit flavor.
Cherry	Cherrywood creates a sweet-tasting smoke flavor that goes wonderfully with pork and poultry. Cherrywood also lends a great color to pork butt and pork shoulder.
Peach	Think of this fruit wood as a milder version of hickory wood. Peach wood is great with a variety of white and pink meats.
Oak	A milder form of hickory, a medium smokey flavor that goes well with all barbecued meats, but especially with beef and pork.

TYPES OF CHARCOAL

When cooking on a charcoal grill or smoker, there are two types of charcoal you can use as your fuel source for the fire: lump charcoal or charcoal briquettes. In some ways, these fuel sources are very similar. After all, briquettes are essentially made from a charcoal; however, they contain binding agents (fancy terminology for chemicals) that help the briquettes hold together and retain their square shape. You might hear some people say that you should always light charcoal briquettes and let them turn gray before you use them to cook. Some people believe that this practice helps burn off some of the binding agents. Similarly, you might also hear some people say that if you place unlit black charcoal briquettes directly on the fire and cook, then the food will obtain a slight chemical flavor. This is most likely a reference to the residual flavor of the binding agents that burn along with the briquettes during the cooking process. Some brands of charcoal briquettes use alternative binding agents, such as cornstarch, and label the product as "natural briquettes." We prefer natural briquettes to standard briquettes, but you should try different brands of charcoal to see what you like best.

People often refer to lump charcoal as being more natural than briquettes because lump charcoal contains no binding agents. Lump charcoal burns at a little hotter temperature than briquettes do, but it usually burns for a slightly shorter duration. Keep this in mind if you start to experiment with lump charcoal.

We think the easiest way to light charcoal is using a Weber charcoal chimney. Our preferred lighting method is to drizzle some cooking oil on a sheet of newspaper, place the newspaper beneath the charcoal chimney, and then light the paper on fire. The cooking oil prolongs the burn time of the newspaper, ensuring the charcoal is lit. One thing we absolutely do not recommend using is charcoal lighter fluid. Lighter fluid is a chemical. Even after the fluid burns off, the chemical residue left behind will leave an unpleasant flavor lingering in the food you cook.

TIME VERSUS TEMPERATURE

One of the things I've learned on the competition circuit is that most cooks usually cook either by time or by temperature. Typically, most competition cooks have so much experience that they accurately estimate how much time a particular piece of meat will take to cook on their smoker. Like anything else, this ability comes with experience. Less experienced cooks often use a meat thermometer during the cooking process to determine how the meat is progressing. Before consuming any meat you cook, it's always a good idea to check it using a meat thermometer for general food safety reasons.

Most of the recipes in this cookbook have references to time and temperature at specific points in the cooking process. One important thing to keep in mind is that meat will cook at different time lengths on different types of smokers. For example, if I provide a recipe and cook using an insulated cabinet, and you make the same recipe using an uninsulated bullet-style cooker, chances are you will have to cook for a slightly longer length of time. In these cases, you should cook with an emphasis on the temperature of the meat, and use a meat thermometer to see how things are coming along. In my opinion, part of what makes cooking outdoors so much fun is gaining the ability to accurately estimate how long something will take to cook. Trust me, after you make a particular recipe a few times, you'll be able to estimate how long the cooking process should take on your smoker, and your friends will admire your cooking skills!

CHAPTER 2

THE BELLY OF THE BEAST

Although pigs provide numerous cuts of meat, including ribs, chops, loins, shoulders and butts, pork belly is one of the most prized sections of the animal. Pork belly comes from the underside of the animal. Essentially, there are five layers to pork belly—three layers of muscle and two layers of fat. Cooked properly, these layers melt together to create a wonderful texture and flavor. Pork belly is often fried, braised or grilled, and is found in a variety of dishes throughout the world.

One of the most celebrated and versatile foods that pigs yield is made from pork belly. That food, arguably one of America's favorites, is bacon. Bacon seems to have a natural way of finding itself on breakfast, lunch and dinner plates in a very complementary and unassuming manner. Similarly, bacon can be covered in chocolate or crumpled into small bits that are hidden in baked goods, transforming them into delectable desserts. Is there any food more adored than bacon? I can't think of one.

A key step in making bacon from pork belly is the curing process. Curing is an ancient food preservation technique that draws away moisture to help prevent spoilage. Two common curing methods are salt curing, also known as corning, and smoke curing. Curing salts contain nitrates. In salt curing, the large amount of salt in conjunction with the nitrates deprives certain bacteria of water, which helps prevent the oxidation process that causes meat to spoil. Similarly, smoke curing helps seal the exterior pores of meat, making the meat more resilient to infection from bacteria. Cured bacon can last in the fridge for about ten days and in the freezer for about three months.

Traditionally, the fatty pieces from a pig's stomach region are cut into strips, cured and then cooked to create the bacon we all know and love. Bacon can also be prepared uncured. Uncured bacon uses natural salts that do not contain nitrates. While uncured bacon is smoked, it won't last long in the fridge and should be consumed within a few days.

This chapter contains instructions on how to cure bacon, plus several recipes I've put together that use bacon as a key ingredient. I hope you enjoy making these recipes as much as I enjoyed creating them—fat wrapped around meat spells *yum!*

PEPPER-CRUSTED PORK BELLY

Pepper-crusted bacon is one of my favorite kinds of bacon. The different types of pepper create a taste that is mildly pungent, a little bit spicy and a fantastic addition to any sandwich.

SERVES: APPROXIMATELY 12–16 • COOK TIME: APPROXIMATELY 3 HOURS

½ cup (144 g) kosher salt

¼ cup (60 g) firmly packed light brown sugar

2 tbsp (12 g) coarsely ground black pepper

¼ cup + 2 tbsp (36 g) coarsely ground mixed peppercorns (pink, green, white and Szechuan)

1 tsp (6 g) curing salt (pink salt)

3-4 lb (1.4-1.8 kg) pork belly, skin off

3-4 chunks hickory wood

In a bowl, combine the kosher salt, brown sugar, black pepper, 2 tablespoons (12 g) mixed peppercorns and curing salt until well mixed.

Put the pork belly in a gallon (3.8 L) zip-top bag with the fat side up. Apply about one-third of the spice mixture, and rub it all over the fat side. Turn the pork belly over. Apply the remaining spice mixture and rub all over the meat side. Seal the bag and put into a full pan. Place the pan in the refrigerator for 6–7 days. Turn over once a day.

After 7 days, remove the pork from the bag and rinse off with cold water. Slice off a small piece, cook and taste. If it is too salty, soak in enough water to cover for 1 hour, and then repeat.

After the pork belly has been rinsed and soaked (if necessary), dry it off and put it back into the pan fat side down; do not cover the pan. Place the pan back into the refrigerator overnight. This process will allow the surface of the meat to form a thin coating called a pellicle, which will allow the smoke to stick to the meat a little better.

For this recipe, I like to use my insulated cabinet smoker. Fire up your smoker to approximately 225°F (107°C). Add the hickory wood just before putting the pork belly on the smoker. If you are using an uninsulated bullet-style cooker (like a WSM), pay attention to the water pan to make sure it doesn't run out of water and cook the belly on the top cooking grate.

Add ¼ cup (24 g) coarsly ground peppercorns to both sides of the pork belly. Cook the pork belly fat side down. You will want to cook this until the internal temperature of the pork belly reaches 150°F (66°C). Typically, this should take about 3 hours.

Remove the pork belly from the smoker and let cool. From this point, you can slice it up and cook it, or wrap it in plastic wrap and store in the fridge for up to 10 days.

MAPLE-SMOKED PORK BELLY

Bacon is salty and maple is sweet. These flavors offset each other, making maple-smoked bacon the perfect combination. This was the very first home-cured bacon recipe I tried. It totally changed my world, and my love for bacon. I thought making bacon at home would be hard, but it was very easy. In fact, the hardest part was patiently waiting out the 7 days for the curing process to finish!

SERVES: APPROXIMATELY 12–16 • COOK TIME: APPROXIMATELY 3 HOURS

FOR THE CURE

½ cup (144 g) kosher salt

½ cup (112 g) packed brown sugar (light or dark)

½ cup (120 ml) real maple syrup

1 tsp (6 g) curing salt (pink salt)

FOR THE SMOKING PROCESS

3–4 lb (1.4–1.8 kg) pork belly, skin off

¼ cup (60 ml) real maple syrup

¼ cup (50 g) maple sugar

2 tbsp (16 g) Smokin' Hoggz All-Purpose Rub (page 181)

3–4 chunks sugar maple wood

To make the cure, place all the ingredients in a small bowl and stir to combine into a paste-like consistency.

For the smoking process, put the pork belly in a gallon (3.8 L) zip-top bag with the fat side up. Apply about one-third of the cure paste, and rub it all over the fat side. Turn the pork belly over. Apply the remaining paste and rub all over the meat side. Seal the bag and put into a full pan. Place the pan in the refrigerator for 6–7 days. Turn over once a day.

After 7 days, remove the pork from the bag and rinse off with cold water. Slice off a small piece, cook and taste. If it is too salty, soak the pork in enough water to cover for 1 hour, and then repeat.

After the pork belly has been rinsed and soaked (if necessary), dry it off and put it back into the pan fat side down; do not cover the pan. Place the pan back into the refrigerator overnight. This process will allow the surface of the meat to form a thin coating called a pellicle, which will allow the smoke to stick to the meat a little better.

In a small bowl, combine the maple syrup, maple sugar and dry rub and apply to the meat side of the pork belly. Rub the ingredients in good so the pork belly is covered evenly.

For this recipe, I like to use my insulated cabinet smoker (Humphrey's Battlebox smoker). Fire up your smoker to approximately 225°F (107°C). If you are using an uninsulated bullet-style cooker (like a WSM), pay attention to the water pan to make sure it doesn't run out of water and cook the belly on the top cooking grate. Add the sugar maple wood to the fire just before putting the pork belly on the smoker.

Cook the pork fat side down. You will want to cook this until the internal temperature of the pork belly reaches 150°F (66°C). Typically, this should take around 3 hours.

Remove the pork belly from the smoker and let cool. Cured bacon can last in the fridge for up to 10 days. Store in the fridge until ready to eat, but I know that it will be hard to wait. After all, we're talking about bacon! Cut yourself off a piece, cook it up and go to your happy place!

MOLASSES AND COFFEE PORK BELLY

This bacon has a nice, rich flavor that only molasses perked up with a little coffee can bring. I've seen recipes using coffee and molasses to brine pork chops, so I asked, "Why not with pork belly?" Well, I think we have a winner here. The coffee provides a background flavor that helps bring out the sweetness of the molasses. Go on, you know you want to give this a try.

SERVES: APPROXIMATELY 12–16 • COOK TIME: APPROXIMATELY 3 HOURS

¾ cup (216 g) kosher salt

¾ cup (175 g) firmly packed dark brown sugar

¼ cup (80 g) molasses

¼ cup (60 ml) very strong brewed coffee or espresso

2 tbsp (12 g) coffee grounds

1 tbsp (6 g) coarsely ground black pepper

1 tsp (6 g) curing salt (pink salt)

3–4 lb (1.4–1.8 kg) pork belly, skin off

3–4 chunks hickory or oak wood

In a bowl, combine the kosher salt, brown sugar, molasses, coffee, coffee grounds, pepper and curing salt to make a paste-like consistency.

Put the pork belly in a gallon (3.8 L) zip-top bag with the fat side up. Apply about one-third of the paste, and rub the paste all over the fat side. Turn the pork belly over. Apply the remaining paste and rub all over the meat side. Seal the bag and put into a full pan. Place the pan in the refrigerator for 6–7 days. Turn over once a day.

After 7 days, remove the pork from the bag and rinse off with cold water. Slice off a small piece, cook and taste. If it is too salty, soak the pork in enough water to cover for 1 hour, and then repeat.

After the pork belly has been rinsed and soaked (if necessary), dry it off and put it back into the pan fat side down; do not cover the pan. Place the pan back into the refrigerator overnight. This process will allow the surface of the meat to form a thin coating called a pellicle, which will allow the smoke to stick to the meat a little better.

For this recipe, I like to use my insulated cabinet smoker. Fire up your smoker to approximately 225°F (107°C). Add the hickory or oak wood just before putting the pork belly on the smoker. If you are using an uninsulated bullet-style cooker (like a WSM), pay attention to the water pan to make sure it doesn't run out of water and cook the belly on the top cooking grate.

Cook the pork belly fat side down. You will want to cook this until the internal temperature of the pork belly reaches 150°F (66°C). Typically, this should take around 3 hours.

Remove the pork belly from the smoker and let cool. From this point, you can slice it up and cook it, or wrap it in plastic wrap and store in the fridge for up to 10 days.

APPLE-SMOKED CURED PORK BELLY

Apple wood gives a slightly sweet flavor to the bacon. In my opinion, this helps set it apart from most of the other hardwood-smoked bacons out there. I kicked this one up a notch by adding some cinnamon, nutmeg and clove during the curing process to create a little more flavor. It'll be like you're eating apple pie, only it's bacon! And who doesn't love bacon?

SERVES: APPROXIMATELY 12–16 • COOK TIME: APPROXIMATELY 3 HOURS

½ cup (144 g) kosher salt

½ cup (120 g) apple butter

¼ cup (60 g) firmly packed brown sugar (light or dark)

1 tbsp (8 g) ground cinnamon

½ tsp ground nutmeg

½ tsp ground cloves

½ tsp allspice

1 tsp (6 g) curing salt (pink salt)

3-4 lb (1.4-1.8 kg) pork belly, skin off

3-4 chunks apple wood

In a bowl, combine the kosher salt, apple butter, brown sugar, cinnamon, nutmeg, cloves, allspice and curing salt to make a paste-like consistency.

Put the pork belly in a gallon (3.8 L) zip-top bag. With the fat side up apply about one-third of the paste, and rub the paste all over fat side. Turn the pork belly over. Apply the remaining paste and rub all over the meat side. Seal the bag and put into a full pan. Place the pan in the refrigerator for 6–7 days. Turn over once a day.

After 7 days, remove the pork from the bag and rinse off with cold water. Slice off a small piece, cook and taste. If it is too salty, soak in enough water to cover for 1 hour, and then repeat.

After the pork belly has been rinsed and soaked (if necessary), dry it off and put it back into the pan fat side down; do not cover the pan. Place the pan back into the refrigerator overnight. This process will allow the surface of the meat to form a thin coating called a pellicle, which will allow the smoke to stick to the meat a little better.

For this recipe, I like to use my insulated cabinet smoker. Fire up your smoker to approximately 225°F (107°C). Add the apple wood just before putting the pork belly on the smoker. If you are using an uninsulated bullet-style cooker (like a WSM), pay attention to the water pan to make sure it doesn't run out of water and cook the belly on the top cooking grate.

Cook the pork fat side down. You will want to cook this until the internal temperature of the pork belly reaches 150°F (66°C). Typically, this should take about 3 hours.

Remove the pork belly from the smoker and let cool. From this point, you can slice it up and cook it, or wrap it in plastic wrap and store in the fridge for up to 10 days.

SAVORY PORK BELLY

This is a great savory bacon recipe that is rich in flavor and would be fantastic to braise and serve as a main course. For an interesting twist, I like to add a little seafood seasoning, such as Old Bay. How many times have you had that on pork? Go on, give this one a try!

SERVES: APPROXIMATELY 12–16 • COOK TIME: APPROXIMATELY 3 HOURS

½ cup (144 g) kosher salt

¼ cup (60 g) firmly packed light brown sugar

2 tbsp (16 g) coarsely ground black pepper

1 tsp (3 g) granulated garlic

1 tsp (2 g) onion powder

½ tsp ground thyme

½ tsp ground celery seed

½ tsp Old Bay Seasoning

1 tsp (6 g) curing salt (pink salt)

3-4 lb (1.4-1.8 kg) pork belly, skin off

3-4 chunks oak wood

In a bowl, combine the kosher salt, brown sugar, pepper, garlic, onion powder, thyme, celery seed, Old Bay and curing salt into a paste-like consistency.

Put the pork belly in a gallon (3.8 L) zip-top bag with the fat side up. Apply about one-third of the paste, and rub it all over the fat side. Turn the pork belly over. Apply the remaining paste and rub all over the meat side. Seal the bag and put into a full pan. Place the pan in the refrigerator for 6–7 days. Turn over once a day.

After 7 days, remove the pork from the bag and rinse off with cold water. Slice off a small piece, cook and taste. If it is too salty, soak in enough water to cover for 1 hour, and then repeat.

After the pork belly has been rinsed and soaked (if necessary), dry it off and put it back into the pan fat side down; do not cover the pan. Place the pan back into the refrigerator overnight. This process will allow the surface of the meat to form a thin coating called a pellicle, which will allow the smoke to stick to the meat a little better.

For this recipe, I like to use my insulated cabinet smoker. Fire up your smoker to approximately 225°F (107°C). Add the oak wood just before putting the pork belly on the smoker. If you are using an uninsulated bullet-style cooker (like a WSM), pay attention to the water pan to make sure it doesn't run out of water and cook the belly on the top cooking grate.

Cook the pork belly fat side down. You will want to cook this until the internal temperature of the pork belly reaches 150°F (66°C). Typically, this should take about 3 hours.

Remove the pork belly from the smoker and let cool. From this point, you can slice it up and cook it, or wrap it in plastic wrap and store in the fridge for up to 10 days.

ASIAN-CURED PORK BELLY

This Asian-cured pork belly is the perfect recipe if you are looking to make some pork belly sliders. The sweetness of the glaze along with the flavors of cinnamon, clove, ginger and allspice really make this pork belly stand out. For the full slider recipe, please see my other cookbook, *Secrets to Smoking*.

SERVES: APPROXIMATELY 12–16 • COOK TIME: APPROXIMATELY 3 HOURS

FOR THE CURE

½ cup (144 g) kosher salt

½ cup (120 ml) mirin

¼ cup (60 g) firmly packed brown sugar (light or dark)

1 tbsp (8 g) ground cinnamon

1 tsp (3 g) Chinese five-spice powder

1 tsp (3 g) ground ginger

1 tsp (3 g) granulated garlic

½ tsp ground cloves

½ tsp allspice

1 tsp (6 g) curing salt (pink salt)

FOR THE SMOKING PROCESS

3-4 lb (1.4-1.8 kg) pork belly, skin off

⅓ cup (80 ml) hoisin sauce

¼ cup (80 g) honey

¼ cup (60 ml) soy sauce

3 tbsp (45 ml) dry sherry

1 tsp (3 g) Chinese five-spice powder

3-4 chunks cherry wood

To make the cure, place all the ingredients in a small bowl and stir to combine into a paste-like consistency.

Place the pork belly in a gallon (3.8 L) zip-top bag with the fat side up. Apply about one-third of the paste, and rub it all over the fat side. Turn the pork belly over. Apply the remaining paste and rub all over the meat side. Seal the bag and put into a full pan. Place the pan in the refrigerator for 6–7 days. Turn over once a day.

After 7 days, remove the pork from the bag and rinse off with cold water. Slice off a small piece, cook and taste. If it is too salty, soak in enough water to cover for 1 hour, and then repeat.

After the pork belly has been rinsed and soaked (if necessary), dry it off and put it back into the pan fat side down; do not cover the pan. Place the pan back into the refrigerator overnight. This process will allow the surface of the meat to form a thin coating called a pellicle, which will allow the smoke to stick to the meat a little better.

For the smoking process, in a bowl, combine the hoisin sauce, honey, soy sauce, sherry and five-spice powder, and apply to the meat side of the pork belly.

For this recipe, I like to use my insulated cabinet smoker. Fire up your smoker to approximately 225°F (107°C). Add the cherry wood just before putting the pork belly on the smoker. If you are using an uninsulated bullet-style cooker (like a WSM), pay attention to the water pan to make sure it doesn't run out of water and cook the belly on the top cooking grate.

Cook the pork belly fat side down. You will want to cook this until the internal temperature of the pork belly reaches 150°F (66°C). Typically, this should take about 3 hours.

Remove the pork belly from the smoker and let cool. From this point, you can slice it up and cook it, or wrap it in plastic wrap and store in the fridge for up to 10 days.

SRIRACHA AND HONEY–CURED PORK BELLY

How about some pork belly with a little yin and yang flavor? The balance between the heat from the Sriracha and the sweetness from the honey gives rise to a delicious harmony of flavors.

SERVES: APPROXIMATELY 12–16 • COOK TIME: APPROXIMATELY 3 HOURS

½ cup (144 g) kosher salt

½ cup (100 g) sugar

1 tsp (6 g) curing salt (pink salt)

¼ cup (60 ml) Sriracha

½ cup (160 g) honey

3–4 lb (1.4–1.8 kg) pork belly, skin off

3–4 chunks mild-flavored smoke wood, such as alder or peach wood

In a bowl, combine the kosher salt, sugar, curing salt, Sriracha and honey into a paste-like consistency.

Put the pork belly in a gallon (3.8 L) zip-top bag with the fat side up. Apply about one-third of the paste, and rub it all over the fat side. Turn the pork belly over. Apply the remaining paste and rub all over the meat side. Seal the bag and put into a full pan. Place the pan in the refrigerator for 6–7 days. Turn over once a day.

After 7 days, remove the pork from the bag and rinse off with cold water. Slice off a small piece, cook and taste. If it is too salty, soak in enough water to cover for 1 hour, and then repeat.

After the pork belly has been rinsed and soaked (if necessary), dry it off and put it back into the pan fat side down; do not cover the pan. Place the pan back into the refrigerator overnight. This process will allow the surface of the meat to form a thin coating called a pellicle, which will allow the smoke to stick to the meat a little better.

For this recipe, I like to use my insulated cabinet smoker. Fire up your smoker to approximately 225°F (107°C). Add the smoke wood just before putting the pork belly on the smoker. If you are using an uninsulated bullet-style cooker (like a WSM), pay attention to the water pan to make sure it doesn't run out of water and cook the belly on the top cooking grate.

Cook the pork belly fat side down. You will want to cook this until the internal temperature of the pork belly reaches 150°F (66°C). Typically, this should take about 3 hours.

Remove the pork belly from the smoker and let cool. From this point, you can slice it up and cook it, or wrap it in plastic wrap and store in the fridge for up to 10 days.

MAPLE-CURED CANADIAN BACON

The cured pork product that Americans know as Canadian bacon is usually called back bacon in other parts of the world. Back bacon is made from the loin cut, which resides in the center of the pig's back. As a result, this bacon is much leaner than conventional bacon. Back bacon is prepared in the same way as conventional bacon, with a salting and smoking process that cures the meat. Usually, a little more sugar is used, lending a sweet quality to Canadian bacon. Typically, Canadian bacon is sliced about ¼-inch (6-mm) thick, and has a texture similar to ham.

SERVES: APPROXIMATELY 8–12 • COOK TIME: APPROXIMATELY 3 HOURS

1 gallon (3.8 L) water, divided

1 cup (288 g) kosher salt

1 cup (240 ml) maple syrup

⅓ cup (80 g) light brown sugar

2 tsp (12 g) curing salt (pink salt)

3 medium cloves garlic, smashed

1 tbsp (6 g) black peppercorns

4-5 lb (1.8-2.3 kg) boneless pork loin, trimmed of excess fat

2-3 chunks sugar maple wood

Combine 1 quart (940 ml) of the water, kosher salt, maple syrup, brown sugar, curing salt, garlic and peppercorns in a medium saucepan. Bring to a boil over high heat, stirring to dissolve the salts and sugar. Boil for 1 minute, and then remove from the heat. Transfer to a large container and stir in the remaining 3 quarts (2.7 L) of water. Place in the refrigerator until completely chilled. Fully submerge the pork loin in the cure, and place in the refrigerator for 3-5 days.

Remove the pork from the cure and place in a large container. Add enough fresh water to fully submerge the loin. Let sit for 30-60 minutes, then remove the pork from the water and pat dry with paper towels.

I will be using my insulated cabinet-style smoker (Humphreys) for this cook. Fire up the smoker to 225°F-250°F (107°C-121°C) and add the sugar maple wood just before you put the pork loin in the smoker. If you are using an uninsulated bullet-style cooker (like a WSM), pay attention to the water pan to make sure it doesn't run out of water and cook the belly on the top cooking grate. Cook until an instant-read thermometer registers 140°F-150°F (60°C-66°C) when inserted into the thickest part of the pork loin, about 2-3 hours.

Remove the pork loin from the smoker and let cool for about 1 hour. When it is cool, slice thinly (about ⅛-inch [3-mm] thick) and pan fry. Serve with some nice fried eggs!

Uncured pork belly is basically pork belly seasoned without the use of curing salts (nitrates). These pork bellies can be marinated or you can use a dry rub seasoning—the choice is yours. I have a couple of uncured belly recipes that use marinades, which I really like and I think you will, too!

APPLE-SMOKED UNCURED PORK BELLY

Apple and pork are a marriage made in heaven, and this recipe confirms that. This recipe uses apple in four ways: apple butter, diced fresh apple, apple cider vinegar and apple wood. If you closed your eyes while eating this you would think you were eating an apple pie. Yeah, it's that good!

SERVES: 8–12 • COOK TIME: APPROXIMATELY 3 HOURS

FOR THE MARINADE

½ cup (120 g) apple butter

¼ cup (150 g) diced apple

¼ cup (60 ml) apple cider vinegar

¼ cup (72 g) kosher salt

¼ cup (60 g) firmly packed light brown sugar

1 tbsp (8 g) ground cinnamon

½ tsp ground nutmeg

FOR THE SMOKING PROCESS

3–4 lb (1.4–1.8 kg) pork belly, skin off

¼ cup (60 g) apple butter

2 tbsp (30 g) light brown sugar

1 tsp (3 g) ground cinnamon

¼ tsp ground nutmeg

3–4 chunks apple wood

To make the marinade, combine all the ingredients in a bowl and keep in the fridge until ready to use. For best results, make the marinade the day before so the ingredients can meld together.

For the smoking process, put the pork belly in a gallon (3.8 L) zip-top bag. Pour the marinade over the pork belly, making sure the whole thing gets covered. Seal the bag and place into a shallow pan. Place the pan in the refrigerator, and let the pork belly marinate for about 2 days. When ready to cook, remove the pork belly from the fridge, rinse it off and pat it dry with a paper towel.

In a small bowl, combine the apple butter, brown sugar, cinnamon and nutmeg. Apply the apple glaze to the meat side. Rub the glaze in good so the meat is nicely covered.

For this recipe, I like to use my insulated cabinet smoker. Fire up your smoker to approximately 225°F (107°C). If you are using an uninsulated bullet-style cooker (like a WSM), pay attention to the water pan to make sure it doesn't run out of water and cook the belly on the top cooking grate. Add the apple wood to the fire just before putting the pork belly on the smoker.

Cook the pork fat side down. You will want to cook this until the internal temperature of the pork belly reaches 150°F (66°C). Typically, this should take about 3 hours.

Remove the pork belly from the smoker and let cool. From this point, you can slice it up and cook it, or wrap it in plastic wrap and store in the fridge for up to 10 days.

MAPLE AND CHIPOTLE UNCURED PORK BELLY

Maple is another flavor that is awesome with pork, especially bacon. To change things up a bit, I decided to add a little smoky spice with some chipotle. Oh boy, am I glad I did! You get a real nice background heat to go along with the great maple flavor.

SERVES: 8–12 • COOK TIME: APPROXIMATELY 3 HOURS

FOR THE MARINADE

½ cup (120 ml) real maple syrup

¼ cup (72 g) kosher salt

¼ cup (50 g) maple sugar

¼ cup (32 g) chipotle powder

FOR THE SMOKING PROCESS

3–4 lb (1.4–1.8 kg) pork belly, skin off

¼ cup (60 ml) real maple syrup

1 tbsp (15 ml) soy sauce

2 tbsp (16 g) chipotle powder

3–4 chunks sugar maple wood

To make the marinade, combine the maple syrup, salt, maple sugar and chipotle powder in a small bowl.

For the smoking process, put the pork belly in a gallon (3.8 L) zip-top bag. Pour the marinade over the pork belly, making sure the whole thing gets covered. Seal the bag and place into a shallow pan. Place the pan in the refrigerator, and let the pork belly marinate for about 2 days. When ready to cook, remove the pork belly from the fridge, rinse it off and pat it dry with a paper towel.

In a small bowl, combine the maple syrup, soy sauce and chipotle powder. Apply the maple-chipotle glaze to the meat side of the pork belly. Rub the glaze in good so the meat is nicely covered.

For this recipe, I like to use my insulated cabinet smoker. Fire up your smoker to approximately 225°F (107°C). If you are using an uninsulated bullet style cooker (like a WSM), pay attention to the water pan to make sure it doesn't run out of water and cook the belly on the top cooking grate. Add the sugar maple wood just before putting the pork belly on the smoker.

Cook the pork fat side down. You will want to cook this until the internal temperature of the pork belly reaches 150°F (66°C). Typically, this should take about 3 hours.

Remove the pork belly from the smoker and let cool. From this point, you can slice it up and cook it, or wrap it in plastic wrap and store in the fridge for up to 10 days.

Pork belly out of smoker resting, ready for slicing.

Slicing pork belly.

Grilling sliced pork belly.

PANCETTA

Pancetta is Italian bacon made from pork belly that is salt-cured and flavored with black pepper and sometimes other spices. For cooking, it is often cut into cubes. It is also thinly sliced and served as a cold cut.

There are two basic types of pancetta, *arrotolata* (rolled) and *stesa* (flat). The *arrotolata* is mainly sliced and used as part of antipasti, while the *stesa* is often chopped and used as an ingredient in many different recipes.

This recipe is for a semi-dry pancetta. After you cure and smoke the pancetta, you must cook it. A fully dried pancetta can be sliced and served after curing and smoking, without cooking it.

SERVES: 15–18 • COOK TIME: APPROXIMATELY 3 HOURS

3 tbsp (24 g) whole black peppercorns, divided

2 tbsp (12 g) whole juniper berries

½ cup (144 g) kosher salt

¼ cup (60 g) dark brown sugar

2 tsp (12 g) curing salt (pink salt)

½ tsp ground nutmeg

3 cloves garlic, minced

4 bay leaves, crushed into tiny pieces

2 tsp (1.5 g) fresh thyme

1 tbsp (2 g) fresh rosemary

5-6 lb (2.3-2.7 kg) pork belly, skin off

2 pieces cheesecloth, larger than the pork belly

Butcher's string

2-3 chunks oak or hickory wood

If you have spice grinder, coarsely grind 2 tablespoons (12 g) of the black peppercorns and the juniper berries. If you don't have a spice grinder, simply place them into a zip-top bag and use a rolling pin to crush them. Place the ground mixture into a bowl with the kosher salt, brown sugar, curing salt, nutmeg, garlic, bay leaves, thyme and rosemary and stir well.

Square up the pork belly to make it look more uniform in shape (square or rectangular). Trim off any excess fat so the entire belly is roughly the same thickness.

After the belly is all trimmed up and looking good, apply the rub to both sides, making sure you get all the corners and edges covered. Then, place the belly into a 2½ gallon (9.5 L) zip-top bag (or use a food saver if you have one). Place in a baking pan and then put the pan into the fridge for 10-14 days. Be sure to turn it once a day.

If, after 10 days, the belly feels a little soft, keep it in the cure for another 3-4 days. It should be firm to the touch, not soft or spongy.

Once the curing is done, take the belly out, rinse it off and then soak it in enough cold water to cover for 1-2 hours to prevent the finished pancetta from tasting too salty.

Move the newly cured pancetta to a clean surface, meat side up. Grind the remaining 1 tablespoon (6 g) peppercorns and rub all over the meat side, making sure to coat the meat evenly.

This step is very important. This step is going to take a little bit of strength because the pancetta at this stage should be firm. Roll the pancetta very tightly into a cylindrical shape, with the fat side facing out, ensuring there are no air pockets. It's crucial to roll the pancetta very tightly! If there are any air gaps, the pancetta will rot. After the pancetta is rolled, wrap it up in 2 sheets of cheesecloth, making sure the cheesecloth is longer than the length of the pancetta. Tie each end with butcher's string to help secure it (kind of like an extra set of hands) while you truss the rest of the belly about every inch (2.5 cm).

PANCETTA (CONTINUED)

Hang the pancetta in a slightly cool, dark, somewhat humid place where air can circulate freely around it. (Ideal conditions are around 60°F [15.6°C] and around 60 percent humidity.) Keep it out of direct sunlight and away from air vents. A basement is ideal, but if you have a second fridge, that will work just fine—just be sure to place a pan of salted water under the hanging pancetta to create a nice moist environment. (Note that there are three main things that will ruin your pancetta during the hanging process: temperatures over 70°F [21°C], too high or too low humidity and direct sunlight.)

Hang the pancetta for about 2 weeks. After the 2 weeks are up, you are now ready for some smokin'!

Fire up your smoker to 200°F-225°F (93°C-107°C). Add the oak or hickory wood just as you are putting the pancetta on the smoker. Leave the wrap on the pancetta and smoke it for 2-3 hours, or until the internal temperature reaches 140°F-150°F (60°C-66°C).

PASTRAMI-CURED PORK BELLY

I don't know about you, but I really enjoy a good pastrami sandwich. With that said, I wanted the best of both worlds—pastrami and bacon. That's when I came up with this pastrami-cured pork belly. What are you waiting for?

SERVES: 8-10 • COOK TIME: APPROXIMATELY 2-3 HOURS

1 gallon (3.8 L) water

¾ cup (216 g) kosher salt

½ cup (100 g) sugar

2 tsp (12 g) curing salt (pink salt)

5 cloves garlic, smashed

2 tbsp (12 g) Pickling Spice (recipe on page 30)

5 lb (2.3 kg) pork belly

1 tbsp (6 g) peppercorns, toasted and ground

1 tbsp (6 g) coriander seed, toasted and ground

2 chunks apple wood

2 chunks hickory wood

In a pot large enough to hold a brisket, combine the water, kosher salt, sugar, curing salt, garlic and pickling spice. Bring to a simmer, stirring until the salt and sugar are dissolved. Remove from the heat and let cool to room temperature, then refrigerate until chilled.

Place pork belly in the brine, weighted with a plate to keep it submerged. Cover and refrigerate for 3 days.

Remove the pork belly from the brine and rinse thoroughly. Refrigerate it for another day uncovered. Combine the peppercorns and coriander and coat the pork belly with the mixture.

For this recipe, I will be using my insulated cabinet smoker (Humphreys). Fire up your smoker to 200°F-225°F (93°C-107°C). If you are using an uninsulated bullet-style cooker (like a WSM), pay attention to the water pan to make sure it doesn't run out of water and cook the belly on the top cooking grate.

Add the apple wood and hickory wood to the fire just before putting the pork belly on the smoker. Cook the pork belly to an internal temperature of 150°F (66°C). Typically, this takes 2-3 hours.

Remove the pork belly from the smoker and let cool. Refrigerate overnight. And because I know you can't wait, feel free to cut off a few of slices and fry them up in a pan!

PICKLING SPICE

2 tbsp (12 g) black peppercorns

2 tbsp (22 g) mustard seeds

2 tbsp (12 g) coriander seeds

2 tbsp (10 g) hot red pepper flakes

2 tbsp (12 g) allspice berries

1 tbsp (7 g) ground mace

2 small cinnamon sticks, crushed or broken into pieces

2–4 bay leaves, crumbled

2 tbsp (12 g) whole cloves

1 tbsp (6 g) ground ginger

Combine the peppercorns, mustard seeds and coriander seeds in a small, dry pan. Place over medium heat and stir until fragrant. Be careful not to burn the ingredients, and keep a lid handy in case seeds pop. Crack the peppercorns and seeds in a mortar and pestle or with the side of a knife on a cutting board. Combine with all the remaining spices. Store in a tightly sealed plastic or glass container.

BRAISED PORK BELLY

If you have never braised uncured pork belly, you are in for a real treat! When done right, the top is nice and crispy and the fat just melts in your mouth. It's so good that you'll want to take a knife and spread that delicious fat on a piece of toast like warm butter. You only live once, so why not, right?

SERVES: APPROXIMATELY 6 • COOK TIME: 4 HOURS

1 cup (240 ml) orange juice

½ cup (120 ml) soy sauce

½ cup (120 g) firmly packed light brown sugar

¼ cup (60 ml) freshly squeezed lemon juice

¼ cup (60 ml) freshly squeezed lime juice

2 tbsp (12 g) minced garlic

2 tbsp (12 g) minced ginger

2 tbsp (10 g) minced green onion

3 lb (1.4 kg) pork belly, uncured and skin off

2 cups (480 ml) chicken stock

In a bowl, combine the orange juice, soy sauce, brown sugar, lemon juice, lime juice, garlic, ginger and green onion and mix until the brown sugar is dissolved.

Place the pork belly in a gallon (3.8 L) zip-top bag and pour the orange juice mixture in. Remove the air from the bag and seal. Place in the fridge for at least 8 hours (overnight would be best).

Remove the pork belly from the fridge and let sit at room temperature for about 1 hour.

Place the pork belly in a disposable aluminum half-pan fat side down and add the chicken stock and marinade from the bag.

For this recipe, I like to use my insulated cabinet smoker (Humphreys). Fire up your smoker to 250°F (121°C). If you are using an uninsulated bullet-style cooker (like a WSM), pay attention to the water pan to make sure it doesn't run out of water and cook the belly on the top cooking grate.

Put the pan with the pork belly in the cooker, cover pan with heavy-duty aluminum foil and cook for 2 hours. Flip the pork belly and cook for another 1½ hours.

Remove from the cooker and place the pan on a cooling rack. Let cool in the braising liquid for about 1½ hours.

Cover with plastic wrap and put in the fridge for about 6 hours or overnight.

Take out of fridge and remove all the congealed fat.

Fire up your charcoal grill for two-zone cooking. Fill up a charcoal chimney with hardwood lump charcoal and light it. When flames start coming out of the top of the chimney, the coals are ready. Dump onto one side of the cooker. Keep the other side clear for indirect cooking. Let the grill get nice and hot.

While the grill is heating up, pour the braising liquid into a pot and bring to a boil over medium-high heat.

Place the pork belly over direct heat and sear for 2–3 minutes on each side. Move the pork belly to the indirect side of the grill, and baste with the heated braising liquid. Cook for about 10 minutes, and baste again. Cook for another 10 minutes, remove from the heat and let rest for 5 minutes. Cut into 6 equal pieces and serve.

APPLE-BACON SLAW

I love a good slaw, and I am always trying new ways to kick things up a little. Here's a dish I love to serve at my parties in the summertime. The Apple-Smoked Cured Pork Belly (page 20) is really the key to this one. What I like to do is make this the day before and let it sit in the fridge overnight so all the ingredients can meld together. When it's just about mealtime, I just stir the slaw around, add the bacon and serve.

SERVES: APPROXIMATELY 6 • PREP TIME: 15 MINUTES

3 tbsp (45 ml) olive oil

1 tbsp (15 ml) apple cider vinegar

¼ cup (60 g) mayonnaise

¼ cup (60 g) sour cream

1 tbsp (16 g) Dijon mustard

1 tbsp (15 ml) lemon juice

½ tsp hot sauce

1 tbsp (12 g) sugar

¼ tsp salt

1 (16-oz [455-g]) package shredded coleslaw mix

1 large apple (any kind), diced

½ lb (227 g) Apple-Smoked Cured Pork Belly (page 20) or other bacon, cooked, crumbled

In a large bowl, combine all the ingredients except the pork belly. Mix well.

If you're serving this right away, after everything is mixed, fold in the bacon, then serve. Otherwise, store in the fridge until ready to use, and then fold in the bacon just before serving.

LOADED-POTATO POTATO SALAD WITH BACON

I remember the first time I had this. I was walking through a small deli and I saw this potato thing sitting in a large bowl in the deli case. I knew I just had to try it! Oh my God, was it ever *so delicious.* I have been trying to replicate that dish, and while I have come close, I've never felt that I quite got there—until my friend Nicole Humphrey made a similar dish, that is. One taste and I said, "This is it!" So here is her recipe for loaded-potato potato salad. Enjoy, and try not to eat the whole thing in one sitting . . . although it will be very tempting!

SERVES: 6–8 • COOK TIME: 10 MINUTES

3 tbsp (45 ml) white vinegar

⅓ cup (55 g) chopped red onion

¾ cup (90 g) chopped celery

½ cup (100 g) chopped bread-and-butter pickles

½ cup (32 g) chopped flat-leaf parsley

½ cup (120 g) mayonnaise

1 tsp (4 g) Dijon mustard

½ tsp ground black pepper

2 lb (910 g) russet potatoes, peeled, cut into ½" (1.3-cm) pieces, cooked, and chilled

3 large hard-boiled eggs, peeled and diced

1 lb (455 g) Pepper-Crusted Pork Belly (page 17) or other bacon, cooked and chopped

1 cup (120 g) shredded cheddar cheese

Combine the white vinegar, onion, celery, pickles, parsley, mayo, mustard and pepper in a large bowl. Add the potatoes and mix well. Fold in the eggs, bacon and cheddar.

BROCCOLI-BACON SALAD

This is the perfect side dish to any summertime cookout or party. It's fresh, delicious and very easy to make. What's great about this dish is you can just as easily make it the day before you need it, so you'll have more time to spend with your guests.

SERVES: APPROXIMATELY 8 • COOK TIME: 10 MINUTES

FOR THE DRESSING

1 cup (240 g) mayonnaise

⅓ cup (65 g) sugar

2 tbsp (30 ml) white vinegar

FOR THE SALAD

6 cups (420 g) broccoli florets

1 cup (160 g) chopped red onion

1 cup (120 g) chopped celery

1 cup (145 g) golden raisins

1 cup (145 g) sunflower seeds

1 lb (455 g) bacon, cooked, drained and crumbled

To make the dressing, combine the mayonnaise, sugar and vinegar in a small bowl. Stir well to blend.

To make the salad, combine the broccoli, onion, celery, raisins and sunflower seeds in a large bowl. Add the dressing and toss until everything is coated nicely. Add the bacon crumbles right before serving.

NOTE: Adding bacon too soon will cause the bacon to become soggy— and nobody wants soggy bacon.

HOMEMADE MAPLE-BACON BUTTER

Making your own butter sounds like a lot of work, but it really isn't. All you need is a couple of ingredients and some sort of food processor, blender or hand mixer. I know, why go through all the trouble, right? Well, because you can't buy this kind of velvety goodness in the stores. In fact, once you make your own, you might hesitate just a little bit the next time you go to purchase butter at the store. What's great about this is you can make all sorts of flavored butters. This maple-bacon butter is one of my favorites and is likely to become a staple ingredient in your refrigerator, too.

MAKES: APPROXIMATELY 2 CUPS (480 G) • COOK TIME: APPROXIMATELY 10 MINUTES

½ lb (227 g) Maple-Smoked Pork Belly (page 18) or other bacon

4 cups (940 ml) heavy cream

¼ cup (60 ml) real maple syrup

Ice water, as needed

NOTE: With a charcoal grill, you can cook using direct heat or indirect heat. For direct heat, simply light the charcoal using a charcoal chimney, and dump the hot coals into the grill. Create a uniform layer of charcoal and cook your food directly above the heat source. For indirect heat, simply light the charcoal using a charcoal chimney, and dump the hot coals into the grill. Stack the charcoal into a single pile on one side of the grill, and cook your food on the opposite side of the grill, away from the heat source.

Pulse the pork belly in your food processor to get nice, tiny pieces. If you don't have a food processor, use a knife to finely dice the bacon. For this recipe, I like to use a standard charcoal grill instead of a smoker. Set up your charcoal grill for direct high-heat cooking (see note), place the pork in a cast-iron pan, place on the grill and fry those little guys until they're crispy. Don't discard the rendered fat. We want that for later on!

Dump all the cream into the bowl of your food processor or a stand mixer (or regular bowl if you're using a hand mixer). Beat that stuff on high while slowly drizzling in your maple syrup, cooked bacon and rendered fat for the first 25 seconds. Using a whisk attachment, continue to beat the cream for 3–6 minutes, until the milk separates from the fat.

This will go through a few stages: whipped cream, then stiff whipped cream, then somewhat of a scrambled egg texture, then all of a sudden the fat will separate. You'll know it's time when your stand mixer starts making a huge mess. I actually keep a towel over the opening of the stand mixer to prevent my counter from being covered in buttermilk. Switch to the paddle attachment at the end, just to coax out that last bit of buttermilk.

Pour off the buttermilk from the fat. You can discard this if you want, but I highly recommend saving it and putting it in pancakes or waffles the next morning. This will be the most delicious buttermilk you'll ever have.

Add ¼ cup (60 ml) ice water (the colder the better) to the butter. Mix the butter around in the water with a fork or a spatula for a minute to rinse the butter of any remaining buttermilk. Discard the water and repeat the process.

Continue to rinse with cold water until the water no longer turns cloudy. By taking out all the buttermilk, it removes the slightly sour taste from the butter, and makes the butter last longer in the fridge.

Pack your butter into your favorite container and feel free to eat it on just about anything you can imagine.

BACON-ONION BALSAMIC JAM

Bacon jam is one of the condiments that adds magnificent flavor to just about any dish you make—from soups and stews to burger toppings, which is one of my favorites. This recipe is easy to make and super delicious. The balsamic vinegar brings this to the next level, slamming your taste buds in bacony bliss.

MAKES: APPROXIMATELY 2 CUPS (480 G) • COOK TIME: APPROXIMATELY 45 MINUTES

8 thick slices Apple-Smoked Cured Pork Belly (page 20) or other bacon, cut into ½" (1.3-cm) pieces

1 large red onion, halved and thinly sliced (about 1½ cups [240 g])

Kosher salt and freshly ground black pepper

⅓ cup (80 ml) water, plus a splash

⅓ cup (80 ml) good-quality balsamic vinegar

1 tsp (4 g) Dijon mustard

Fire up your charcoal grill for direct-heat cooking. Simply light the charcoal using a charcoal chimney, and dump the hot coals into the grill. Create a uniform layer of charcoal and cook your food directly above the heat source.

Heat a large cast-iron sauté pan (use one that has a cover, or use heavy-duty aluminum foil if no cover can be found). Add the bacon and cook, stirring occasionally, until browned but not crispy, about 10 minutes. Remove the bacon from the pan and let it drain on a paper towel. Drain off all but ¼ cup (60 ml) of the bacon grease and then stir in the onion, about ¼ teaspoon salt and a pinch of pepper. Cover the pan and cook the onions for 5 minutes. Uncover the pan and add in a splash of water, scraping the bits off the bottom of the pan with a spatula or wooden spoon. Continue to cook the onions for 10 minutes, stirring occasionally, until they are soft and lightly browned.

After the onions have cooked for 10 minutes, stir in the balsamic vinegar, mustard and remaining ⅓ cup (80 ml) water, and then return the bacon to the pan and bring the mixture to a simmer. Simmer, uncovered, until the sauce thickens and is almost completely absorbed, about 5 minutes. At this point, the jam can be covered and refrigerated (you can make it up to 2 days in advance). If using immediately, set it aside in a bowl until ready to use.

BACON WEAVE

Ah, the bacon weave. This is something that those who love bacon really need to have in their arsenal. A bacon weave cooks flat and evenly. Not only is the bacon weave great for wrapping chicken, meatloaf and sausage fatties, but it's also great in sandwiches to ensure you get bacon in every bite! Here, I am going to show you the fine art of creating a bacon weave. For ways to use the bacon weave, see pages 45-46.

SERVES: APPROXIMATELY 4 • COOK TIME: 30–45 MINUTES

16 slices (about 1 lb [455 g]) bacon

Lay 8 strips of bacon vertically across a rimmed baking sheet or aluminum foil, flush against each other. Fatty sides should all face one direction and meaty sides should all face the other direction. The width should match the length of the strips.

Fold every other strip in half onto itself. Lay one strip of bacon perpendicular to those strips, flush against the back of the folds. Unfold those flipped strips back over the perpendicular strip of bacon.

Now fold every other strip in the alternating columns. Lay one strip of bacon perpendicular to those strips, flush against the back of the folds. Unfold those strips back down over the perpendicular strip of bacon.

Repeat again with the first set of strips. Do the same thing on the upper half of the weave. There should be the same number of strips going down as there are going across.

Cooking time and temperature will vary depending on what meat you're wrapping the weave around. To cook as is, heat a smoker to 350°F (177°C) and cook for 30–45 minutes. The dish is usually done cooking when the bacon tightens around the meat and adheres in place.

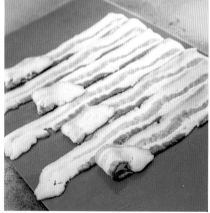
Folding back every other strip.

Laying bacon across.

Making checkerboard pattern.

Seasoning finished bacon weave.

BACON WEAVE BREAKFAST BURRITO

Breakfast is my favorite meal of the day. For me, anything goes—from cold pizza to steak and eggs—but one of my all-time faves is a breakfast burrito with eggs, bacon, sausage, cheese and hash browns. You can put anything you want in it—the sky is the limit. Here's a little twist on this all-time classic: I am going to use bacon as my outside shell. What? Yup, you heard it here first! Breakfast will never be the same again.

SERVES: 2 • COOK TIME: APPROXIMATELY 1–1½ HOURS

1 Bacon Weave (page 42)

1 cup (110 g) cooked hash browns

2 tbsp (30 ml) hot sauce

4 eggs, scrambled

4 breakfast sausage links

½ cup (60 g) shredded cheddar or pepper Jack cheese

¼ cup (60 g) chunky salsa (mild, medium or hot)

1 chunk apple wood

For this recipe, I like to use my insulated cabinet smoker. Fire up your smoker to 275°F–300°F (135°C–150°C). If you are using an uninsulated bullet-style cooker (like a WSM), pay attention to the water pan to make sure it doesn't run out of water and cook the belly on the top cooking grate.

Lay out your Bacon Weave on a sheet of heavy-duty aluminum foil. Add the hash browns and top with hot sauce. Next add the scramble egg, breakfast sausage, cheddar cheese and salsa. Roll it up and make sure the seam ends up on the bottom. This will help ensure that the burrito stays together while you're cooking it.

Add the apple wood just before putting the meat on the smoker. Place on the smoker seam side down and cook until the bacon is done and browned, 1–1½ hours.

Remove and let sit for about 10 minutes, and then cut in half and serve.

Drizzling hot sauce over hash browns.

Adding egg, cheese, sausage and salsa.

Folding weave around filling.

BACON WEAVE QUESADILLA

What's a Bacon Weave Quesadilla? It's a quesadilla with bacon in place of the tortilla shell. Let me repeat that for ya: a quesadilla with bacon in place of the tortilla shell. Think about melty cheese, smoky chicken, chunky salsa and spicy jalapeños melding into the crispy bacon layer. Now let your taste buds be happy!

SERVES: 4 • COOK TIME: APPROXIMATELY 15 MINUTES

2 Bacon Weaves (page 42), precooked

½ cup (60 g) shredded cheddar cheese

1 lb (455 g) chicken, cooked and sliced about ½" (1.3-cm) thick

1 cup (160 g) thinly sliced cooked onion

1 cup (150 g) thinly sliced cooked red and green peppers

½ cup (60 g) shredded Monterey Jack cheese

½ cup (120 g) queso fresco (Mexican cheese)

1 cup (240 g) chunky salsa

¼ cup (60 g) diced jalapeños

1 cup (240 g) sour cream

½ cup (50 g) sliced green onion

Lay out one of the bacon weaves and cover with cheddar cheese. Add the chicken, onion, peppers, Monterey Jack, queso fresco, salsa and jalapeños, then top with the other bacon weave.

Fire up your charcoal grill for two-zone cooking. Fill up a charcoal chimney with hardwood lump charcoal and light it. When flames start coming out of the top of the chimney, the coals are ready. Dump onto one side of the cooker. Keep the other side clear for indirect cooking.

Place the quesadilla on a piece of heavy-duty aluminum foil, and then place the foil onto the cooking grates. Cook on the indirect side of the grill for about 10–15 minutes, until the cheese is melted. You may want to spin it 180 degrees after about 5–7 minutes so it will cook evenly. Once the cheese has melted, remove from the grill and let sit for about 5 minutes.

Cut into squares and serve with the sour cream and green onions.

Placing bacon weave on top of mixture.

Quesadilla ready for cooking.

BACON-WRAPPED CHICKEN WINGS WITH BOURBON BARBECUE SAUCE

Chicken wings are a great party food, but sometimes they can get a little boring. Why not mix things up a little bit by wrapping the wings in bacon and then tossing them in a sticky, sweet bourbon barbecue sauce?

SERVES: APPROXIMATELY 6 • COOK TIME: APPROXIMATELY 1½ HOURS

¼ tsp freshly cracked pepper

3 lb (1.4 kg) chicken wings (24 wings, separate drummettes from wings)

12 slices bacon, any kind, cut in half

2 chunks sugar maple wood

2 cups (480 ml) Bourbon Barbecue Sauce (page 174)

For this recipe, I like to use my insulated cabinet smoker. Fire up your smoker to 300°F (150°C). If you are using an uninsulated bullet-style cooker (like a WSM), pay attention to the water pan to make sure it doesn't run out of water and cook the belly on the top cooking grate.

Sprinkle the pepper over the chicken. Wrap each chicken wing with a half-slice of bacon.

Add the sugar maple wood just before you put the wings on. Place the bacon-wrapped chicken wings onto the cooking grate, with the bacon seam side down. Cook for about 1½ hours, or until golden brown and the juice of the chicken runs clear when the thickest part is cut to the bone (the meat should reach an internal temperature of at least 165°F [74°C]). Remove from the cooker.

In a large bowl, toss the chicken with half of the sauce. Serve warm with the remaining sauce on the side for dipping.

Finished wrapping wings with bacon and starting to season.

Finished seasoning wings.

Basting with sauce.

BACON-WRAPPED ONION RINGS

People are always saying you have to eat more veggies, right? Well, here is your chance. Can life get any better than this? Bacon-wrapped onion rings, with sweetness from the onion and smokiness from the bacon, cooked to perfection. I'll be surprised if you don't eat the whole plate!

SERVES: 4–8 • COOK TIME: APPROXIMATELY 1½ HOURS

FOR THE SRIRACHA MAYO DIPPING SAUCE

½ cup (120 g) mayonnaise

2 tbsp (30 ml) Sriracha

2 tsp (10 ml) lime juice

½ tsp paprika

Salt and pepper to taste

FOR THE ONION RINGS

2 large sweet onions

Dry rub of your choice, such as Smokin' Hoggz All-Purpose Rub (page 181)

2 lb (910 g) thinly sliced bacon, any kind

2–3 chunks apple wood or peach wood

Smokin' Hoggz Barbecue Sauce or your favorite barbecue sauce

To make the Sriracha mayo, combine all the ingredients in a small bowl. Refrigerate until ready to use.

To make the onion rings, cut the onions into rings about ½-inch (1.3-cm) thick and separate each ring. Lay them out on a flat surface and dust them lightly with the dry rub. Wrap a slice of bacon around the onion ring; for the smaller rings you may be able to use a half-slice of bacon. Secure the bacon on the onion with a skewer or toothpick.

For this recipe, I like to use a non-insulated bullet-style cooker, and set it up for 275°F–300°F (135°C–149°C). Use the top grate to cook on as the temperature will be a little hotter than the bottom grate. Add the apple wood or peach wood to the cooker just before you put the onion rings on. Cook for about 1½ hours. When the bacon is done, brush with the barbecue sauce and continue to cook an additional 15 minutes to set the sauce.

If you are going to use your charcoal grill for this, set it up for two-zone cooking. Fill up a charcoal chimney with hardwood lump charcoal and light it. When flames start coming out of the top of the chimney, the coals are ready. Dump onto one side of the cooker. Keep the other side clear for indirect cooking. Add the smoke wood to the cooker just before you put the onion rings on. Place the wrapped onion rings on the grate directly over the coals and sear them for about 1 minute per side, then move them to the cooler side of the grill for about 1 hour, or until the bacon is cooked. When the bacon is done, brush with the barbecue sauce and continue to cook an additional 15 minutes to set the sauce.

Remove from the cooker and serve with the Sriracha mayo.

BACON-WRAPPED STUFFED SHRIMP

Let's see . . . bacon, shrimp, cream cheese and jalapeño. Yeah, I can already see your mouth watering! This dish will prove to be such a delicious little treat that your friends and family will be begging for more.

SERVES: 6 (2 SHRIMP PER PERSON) • COOK TIME: APPROXIMATELY 30 MINUTES

12 thin slices bacon, any kind

8 oz (225 g) cream cheese, softened

½ cup (70 g) diced jalapeños

¼ cup (60 ml) sweet chili sauce

12 super colossal shrimp (U-12, approximately 12 shrimp per lb [455 g]), peeled and deveined, tail on

½ cup (120 ml) Smokin' Hoggz Barbecue Sauce or Honey BBQ Sauce (page 173)

Fire up your charcoal grill for two-zone cooking. Fill up a charcoal chimney with hardwood lump charcoal and light it. When flames start coming out of the top of the chimney, the coals are ready. Dump the hot coal onto one side of the grill. Keep the other side clear for indirect cooking.

Coat a sheet of heavy-duty foil with nonstick cooking spray. Lay the bacon out on top of it. Place the foil on the grill and cook using the indirect method. Cook the bacon about halfway, which usually takes about 10 minutes. Do not cook the bacon all the way through; you want it to be flexible so you can wrap it around the shrimp.

In a bowl, combine the cream cheese, jalapeños and sweet chili sauce and mix well. Set aside until ready to use.

Using a small paring knife, butterfly the shrimp. Start from the inside curve down by the tail and go all the way to the other end. Slice as deep as possible without cutting all the way through. The reason I like to butterfly from the inside of the curve is that it gives you a natural pouch to add your stuffing.

Stuff about 2 tablespoons (30 g) of the filling into the center of each shrimp. Wrap one piece of bacon around the stuffed shrimp and secure it in place with a toothpick. Repeat for the remaining shrimp.

Place the shrimp on to the indirect heat zone on the grill. Cook until the shrimp are done, about 10 minutes. Brush with barbecue sauce. If you want the bacon to be a little crunchier, finish the shrimp on the direct-heat side of the grill for about 2 minutes per side.

BACON AND EGGNOG COCKTAIL

Eggnog has been a family tradition around the Christmas holidays ever since I can remember. It's usually the same old thing, so it can get sort of boring, right? Well, here's a little twist to spruce up the cocktail and make the holiday festive again. Note that the bourbon takes several days to infuse with the bacon, so plan accordingly.

SERVES: APPROXIMATELY 8 • PREP TIME: 15 MINUTES

FOR THE BACON-INFUSED BOURBON

1 (750 ml) bottle bourbon (I like Bulleit bourbon, but use whatever you like)

¼ cup (60 ml) warm bacon grease

FOR THE EGGNOG

½ gallon (1.8 L) prepared eggnog

1½ cups (355 ml) bacon-infused bourbon

8 slices bacon, any kind, cooked

8 cinnamon sticks

Grated nutmeg

Pour out ¼ cup (60 ml) of the bourbon from the bottle and enjoy it however you enjoy your bourbon. Pour the warm bacon grease into the bottle. Cover and let stand for 4 hours, shaking the bottle occasionally. Chill for 3–7 days.

Pour the bourbon through a wire-mesh strainer lined with a coffee filter into a bowl. Discard the filter. Clean the bottle. Pour the strained bourbon back into the bottle, and store at room temperature for up to 6 months.

In a pitcher, combine the eggnog and bacon-infused bourbon and stir until well mixed. Divide among 8 (7-ounce [210-ml]) bourbon glasses and garnish each with a slice of bacon, a cinnamon stick and a little grated nutmeg.

BACON-WRAPPED PINEAPPLE MOZZARELLA RINGS

I saw this recipe done by Harry Soo (he's big on the competition barbecue circuit) and I just had to try it. Holy cow (I mean pig), was it good! The saltiness of the bacon, the sweetness of the pineapple and the gooeyness of the cheese—what's not to love, right? Here is my take on Harry's recipe.

SERVES: 4 • COOK TIME: APPROXIMATELY 45 MINUTES

2 large Vidalia or sweet yellow onions

8 slices canned pineapple rings, juice drained and reserved

8 mozzarella string cheese sticks

24 slices bacon (your choice, but for this one, I like the Sriracha and Honey-Cured Pork Belly, page 23)

¼ cup (32 g) Smokin' Hoggz All-Purpose Rub (page 181)

1 cup (240 g) Smokin' Hoggz Barbecue Sauce or your favorite barbecue sauce

Peel and cut the onions into ½-inch (1.3-cm) slices.

Match the onion rings to the size of the pineapple slices—choose rings that have more of a bowl shape to help hold the string cheese in place.

Tear the mozzarella string cheese in half lengthwise.

Place one half of the mozzarella in the onion ring and cut the other half to fill in the remaining gap.

Wrap the pineapple ring, onion ring and mozzarella with 3 bacon strips per ring. Secure with toothpicks. Sprinkle on the dry rub.

Start up your charcoal grill for two-zone cooking. Fill up a charcoal chimney with hardwood lump charcoal and light it. When flames start coming out of the top of the chimney, the coals are ready. Dump onto one side of the grill. Keep the other side clear for indirect cooking. Heat to 400°F (204°C). Cook over indirect heat for 30–45 minutes.

Brush with the barbecue sauce, and cook an additional 10 minutes so the sauce can set. Remove and let cool for a few minutes before serving.

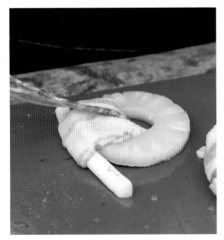
Wrapping with bacon.

Continuing wrapping with bacon.

Basting with sauce.

PIG SHOTS

These Pig Shots are the perfect addition to your next party or tailgate. The reason they're called Pig Shots is that once assembled, they look like a shot glass made from bacon that is filled with cream cheese! They are wicked easy to make and can be prepared the day before. This recipe calls for sweet Italian sausage, but if you like things a little spicier like I do, then try using hot Italian sausage.

MAKES: 24–30 • COOK TIME: 1½–2 HOURS

1 lb (455 g) sweet Italian sausage (or hot Italian sausage if you like it spicy)

1 lb (455 g) thick-cut bacon, any kind

8 oz (225 g) cream cheese, at room temperature

4 tbsp (32 g) Smokin' Hoggz All-Purpose Rub (page 181)

1 cup (240 g) firmly packed brown sugar (light or dark)

Barbecue sauce or real maple syrup (optional)

Cut the sausage into slices ⅓–½ inch (8–13 mm) thick.

Cut the bacon in half lengthwise, then wrap a half strip around each sausage slice, using a toothpick to pin it closed and form the shot glass.

In a bowl, combine the cream cheese and 1 tablespoon (8 g) of the rub. Fill a piping bag with the cream cheese mixture, and then pipe the cream cheese into each Pig Shot, leaving a bit of room at the top.

Top each Pig Shot with a spoonful of brown sugar and a sprinkling of the rub.

I will be using my uninsulated bullet-style smoker (WSM) for this cook. Fire up the smoker to 275°F (135°C). Cook the pig shots in a disposable aluminum half-pan for 1½–2 hours, until the bacon is nice and firm.

For a slight glaze and a little sweetness, you can brush on some of your favorite barbecue sauce or maple syrup during the last 15 minutes of cooking.

CORNBREAD-STUFFED BACON-WRAPPED SHRIMP

Shrimp is one of those foods from the ocean that I think is very versatile. As Bubba Gump of the Bubba Gump Shrimp Company said, you can fry it, grill it, bake it, smoke it, stuff it, put it in soups or stews and more. Here, I'm going to show you a really easy and delicious way to stuff shrimp and then wrap it in bacon. I like how the sweetness of the cornbread contrasts with the salty, smoky bacon.

SERVES: 6 • COOK TIME: APPROXIMATELY 30 MINUTES

12 thin slices bacon, any kind

12 super colossal shrimp (U-12, approximately 12 shrimp per lb [455 g]), peeled and deveined, tail on

3 cups (420 g) Chourico and Cornbread Stuffing (page 88) or your favorite cornbread stuffing

¼ cup (32 g) Smokin' Hoggz All-Purpose Rub (page 181)

1 cup (240 ml) Smokin' Hoggz Barbecue Sauce or your favorite barbecue sauce

Fire up your charcoal grill for two-zone cooking. Fill up a charcoal chimney with hardwood lump charcoal and light it. When flames start coming out of the top of the chimney, the coals are ready. Dump onto one side of the cooker. Keep the other side clear for indirect cooking.

Coat a sheet of heavy-duty foil with nonstick cooking spray. Lay the bacon out on the foil. Place the foil on the grill on the indirect heat zone. Cook the bacon about halfway, which usually takes about 10 minutes. Do not cook the bacon all the way through; you want the bacon to be flexible so you can wrap it around the shrimp.

Using a small paring knife, butterfly the shrimp. Start from the inside curve down by the tail and go all the way to the other end. Slice as deep as possible without cutting all the way through. The reason I like to butterfly from the inside of the curve is it gives you a natural pouch to add your stuffing.

Stuff about ¼ cup (32 g) of the filling into the center of each shrimp, wrap 1 piece of bacon around the stuffed shrimp, and secure it in place with a toothpick. Sprinkle a little dry rub on the shrimp. Repeat for the remaining shrimp and bacon.

Place the shrimp on the indirect heat zone on the grill. Cook until the shrimp turn white and are done, about 10 minutes, then brush with the barbecue sauce. If you want the bacon to be a little crunchier, finish the shrimp on the direct heat side of the grill for about 2 minutes per side.

PORK BELLY REUBEN

I love a good Reuben sandwich, but why not mix things up a little? I have created my own Reuben sandwich using pork belly instead of corned beef. I like how the spicy, peppery heat of the Sriracha mixes with the salty, smoky textures of the pork belly. Everything else stays the same, but the pork belly is the sole star in this one, and it certainly brings the sandwich up a few notches, as far as I'm concerned!

SERVES: 2 • COOK TIME: APPROXIMATELY 20–25 MINUTES

½ sweet onion, julienned

1 lb (455 g) sauerkraut, drained and rinsed

½ cup (120 ml) Thousand Island dressing

1-2 tbsp (15-30 ml) Sriracha (depending on how spicy you like it)

4 slices dark rye bread

4 slices Swiss cheese

6 thick slices (½" [1.3-cm] thick) Pastrami-Cured Pork Belly (page 29), cooked

4 tbsp (56 g) butter

Set up your grill for two-zone cooking. Fill up a charcoal chimney with hardwood lump charcoal and light it. When flames start coming out of the top of the chimney, the coals are ready. Dump onto one side of the cooker. Keep the other side clear for indirect cooking.

Start heating up a cast-iron skillet. Once heated, add the onion and cook for about 5 minutes. When the onion starts to turn color, add the sauerkraut and continue to cook for another 5 minutes.

In a small bowl, mix together the Thousand Island dressing and Sriracha. Spread about 2 tablespoons (30 ml) of the dressing on 2 slices of rye bread. Place 1 slice of cheese on top of the dressing. Add 3 slices of pork belly and enough of the sauerkraut and onion mixture to cover the pork belly. Place a last slice of cheese on top and add the remaining slices of bread to make 2 sandwiches.

Spread 1 tablespoon (15 g) of butter on each side of the sandwich and place the sandwiches in the skillet. Grill for 2-3 minutes per side over direct heat. Move the sandwich to the indirect side of the grill and finish cooking for about 5 more minutes, until the bread is nicely toasted and the cheese is melted.

Remove the sandwiches from the grill, cut in half and serve with the remaining Thousand Island dressing.

BACON, BANANA AND PEANUT BUTTER SANDWICH

Elvis has just reentered the building. The King, whose favorite sandwich was banana and peanut butter, would be proud of this one! The crispy bacon adds a hint of crunch to the softness of the sandwich.

SERVES: 4 • COOK TIME: 5–7 MINUTES

8 pieces thick-cut Texas Toast

1 cup (260 g) all-natural chunky peanut butter (I like Teddie brand)

½ cup (120 g) pepper jelly

4 medium bananas

16 pieces thick-cut Maple-Smoked Pork Belly (page 18), cooked

½ cup (112 g) butter, softened

Set up your charcoal grill for two-zone cooking. Fill up a charcoal chimney with hardwood lump charcoal and light it. When flames start coming out of the top of the chimney, the coals are ready. Dump onto one side of the cooker. Keep the other side clear for indirect cooking. Start heating up a cast-iron skillet.

To assemble the sandwiches, lay out 2 pieces of Texas Toast. Spread ¼ cup (65 g) of peanut butter on one side and about 2 tablespoons (30 g) of pepper jelly on the other side. Slice up 1 banana and place the slices on the peanut butter side of the sandwich. Put 4 pieces of bacon on top of the banana slices. Place the second piece of toast on top, jelly side down. Repeat for the other 3 sandwiches. Spread 1 tablespoon (14 g) of softened butter on each side of the sandwiches.

Place a sandwich in the cast-iron skillet. Cook for about 3 minutes, or until it's a nice golden-brown color. Flip over and do the same for the other side. Depending on the size of your pan, you may be able to cook 2 sandwiches at one time.

When the sandwiches are cooked, cut each in half on the diagonal and serve with a nice glass of ice cold milk!

Adding layer of banana.

Topping with bacon.

Cooking in cast-iron pan.

BACON CORN CHOWDER

Fall is one of those bittersweet times of the year for me. One, you have some warm days and cool nights, which is great for sleeping. Two, there is the scenic changing of the leaves, which is always nice to see. Three, winter is right around the corner, so you know the cold and snow are coming (I'm not a big fan of snow anymore). Four, I get to make all kinds of soups, stews and chowders! One thing I love to do is get fresh corn in August or September, remove the kernels and freeze them so I can make corn chowder during the late fall and early winter. This is a great dish for a cool fall Sunday afternoon. The peppered bacon really makes this dish pop. It's even better for lunch the next day—that is, if there's any left.

SERVES: APPROXIMATELY 6–8 • COOK TIME: APPROXIMATELY 2–3 HOURS

1 lb (455 g) Pepper-Crusted Pork Belly (page 17) or any bacon, diced

1 shallot, finely diced

1 clove garlic, minced

2 tsp (6 g) chili powder

1 tbsp (8 g) dry mustard powder

2 tbsp (16 g) flour

2½ cups (590 ml) low-sodium chicken stock

3 large red potatoes, cut into ½" (1.3-cm) cubes

2 cups (470 ml) whole milk

1 cup (240 ml) light cream

2 cups (280 g) diced ham

6 cups (900 g) freshly cut corn from the cob

I like to use my charcoal grill for this recipe, and I set it up for two-zone cooking. Fill up a charcoal chimney with hardwood lump charcoal and light it. When flames start coming out of the top of the chimney, the coals are ready. Dump onto one side of the cooker. Keep the other side clear for indirect cooking.

Place a cast-iron Dutch oven on the cooking grate directly over the coals to start heating the pan. Add the bacon and cook for 10–15 minutes, until the bacon is crispy. Remove the bacon and set aside, keeping the bacon grease in the pan.

Next add the shallot, garlic, chili powder and mustard powder and cook for 5 minutes, until the shallots are translucent.

Now add the flour and whisk until a nice golden brown, 5–10 minutes. Once it's golden brown, you can add the chicken stock. Whisk until it's mixed well, and then bring to a simmer.

Add in the potatoes and let cook for about 15 minutes. Then add in the milk and light cream. Mix and bring up to simmer, about 10 minutes. Now add the cooked bacon, ham and corn.

Set the pot on the cooler zone of the grill. Cover the pot and put the lid on the grill. Cook for 1½–2 hours, making sure to add more charcoal if needed.

When the chowder is done, let it rest for about 30 minutes. Serve in a bowl and enjoy!

TATER TOTS WITH BACON CASSEROLE

Who doesn't love tater tots? I certainly do, and every time I have them it instantly sends me back to my childhood! Remember having plate after plate of these delicious crispy potato nuggets? What's better than tater tots? How about a tater tot casserole with bacon and gooey cheese? Now sit back and enjoy this little ride down memory lane.

SERVES: APPROXIMATELY 8 • COOK TIME: APPROXIMATELY 1–1½ HOURS

1 (2-lb [910-g]) package tater tots, cooked according to package directions

½ cup (80 g) diced Vidalia or sweet onion

½–1 cup (120–240 ml) hot sauce, such as Frank's RedHot (more or less, depending on how hot you like it)

16 oz (455 g) shredded cheddar cheese

1 Bacon Weave (page 42)

½ lb (225 g) bacon, any type, cooked and crumbled

In a bowl, combine the cooked tater tots, onion, hot sauce and cheese.

Place the Bacon Weave into the bottom of a disposable half-pan. Add the tater tot mixture and top with the crumbled bacon.

For this recipe, I like to use a non-insulated bullet-style smoker, and set it up to cook at 325°F (163°C). You can use any smoker you want for this recipe, but I like the non-insulated smoker because it's a quick cook and I don't need a lot of fuel.

Place the casserole on the top shelf and cook for 1–1½ hours, or until the Bacon Weave is cooked.

Remove from the cooker when done, cover loosely with aluminum foil, and let rest for 15–20 minutes. Once cool, flip the casserole over so the weave is on top. Cut into squares and serve.

SWEET POTATO AND BACON HASH

I wanted to try something a little different than the traditional corned beef hash dish. I had a couple of Japanese sweet potatoes lying around, along with some bacon and onions. I whipped up a little something for breakfast, and *oh man!* I don't know if I'll ever go back to regular corned beef hash again.

SERVES: 4 • COOK TIME: 30–45 MINUTES

2 Japanese sweet potatoes

2 tbsp (30 ml) olive oil

2 tbsp (16 g) Smokin' Hoggz All-Purpose Rub (page 181)

1 lb (455 g) Pepper-Crusted Pork Belly (page 17) or any bacon, cut into ¼" (6-mm) cubes

1 shallot, diced

Set up your charcoal grill for two-zone cooking. Fill up a charcoal chimney with hardwood lump charcoal and light it. When flames start coming out of the top of the chimney, the coals are ready. Dump onto one side of the cooker. Keep the other side clear for indirect cooking.

Peel the sweet potatoes and cut them into ¼-inch (6-mm) cubes. Place in a bowl, add the olive oil and mix to coat, then lightly season with the rub.

Place a cast-iron skillet over the direct-heat zone to heat it up. Add the bacon. If the pan starts to get too hot, move it to the indirect-heat zone. Cook the bacon until almost done, 10–15 minutes. Remove from the pan and set aside.

Leave about 2–3 tablespoons (30–45 ml) of bacon grease in the pan, add the shallot and cook for 3–5 minutes. Add the sweet potato, and cook until the potatoes are almost soft (15–20 minutes). Add the bacon back to the pan and finish cooking for 5–10 minutes.

WHOLE-BELLY PORCHETTA

If you have never heard of or had porchetta, you don't know what you're missing! In my opinion, this is one of the greatest dishes ever created. Basically, porchetta is an old Italian tradition of taking a huge piece of pork (the belly), stuffing it with herbs and spices, rolling it up into a large meat log and cooking it in the oven to perfection. You can slice it thin and serve it in a sandwich or just enjoy it by itself. Either way, you won't be disappointed with this porky goodness.

SERVES: APPROXIMATELY 20–30 • COOK TIME: APPROXIMATELY 5 HOURS

¼ cup (24 g) fennel seeds

¼ cup (20 g) red pepper flakes

2 tbsp (12 g) black peppercorns

¼ cup (10 g) minced fresh sage

2 tbsp (4 g) minced fresh rosemary

8 cloves garlic, minced

Zest of 1 lemon

10–12 lb (4.6–5.5 kg) full-size fresh pork belly, skin off

Kosher salt to taste

Cracked black pepper

4 good-size chunks apple wood

2 (12-oz [355-ml]) cans beer, your choice (I use Pabst Blue Ribbon)

Toast the fennel seeds, red pepper flakes and peppercorns in a small skillet over medium heat until fragrant, about 1 minute. Transfer the spices to a bowl and let cool. Grind the spices to a medium grind in a spice mill and transfer to a small bowl. Add the sage, rosemary, garlic and lemon zest. Set the mixture aside.

Place the belly on your work surface skin side down. Arrange it so the loin is in the center. Using a knife, score the belly flesh in a checkerboard pattern ½-inch (1.3-cm) deep so it will cook evenly. Generously salt the belly; rub with the fennel mixture.

Roll up tightly and tie crosswise with butcher's twine at ½-inch (1.3-cm) intervals.

Refrigerate the belly, uncovered, for 1 day to allow the seasonings to do their thing and flavor the pork. Let the porchetta sit at room temperature for about 1 hour. Season the outside of the porchetta with kosher salt and cracked black pepper. Cut the porchetta in half; this will allow for a more even cook and ensure it will fit it into your smoker.

For this recipe, I like to use my insulated cabinet smoker (Humphrey's). I like using this for long cooks because of the consistent temperatures I get throughout the cooking period. Fire up your cooker to 275°F (135°C). If you are using an uninsulated bullet-style cooker (like a WSM), pay attention to the water pan to make sure it doesn't run out of water and cook the belly on the top cooking grate.

Add the apple wood chunks just before putting the porchetta on the smoker. Place the porchetta near the top and cook until an instant-read thermometer inserted into the center of the meat registers 160°F (71°C). It should take 2–3 hours.

Place the porchetta into a full-size disposable aluminum pan, add the beer and cover with heavy-duty aluminum foil. Place back into the cooker and cook for an additional 2–3 hours, until the internal temperature reaches 190°F (88°C).

Remove and let rest for 30 minutes. Remove the butcher's twine. Using a serrated knife, slice into ¼-inch (6-mm) rounds.

CHOCOLATE BACON BARK

Okay, even though this recipe doesn't call for a smoker to be used, I had to add it anyway. I think this recipe is way too good not to share with you! This chocolate bacon goodness will totally satisfy your sweet tooth, but be careful, 'cause you just may end up eating the whole darn thing and not sharing any of it with anyone else!

MAKES: 16 PIECES

16 oz (455 g) semisweet chocolate morsels

4 cups (280 g) mini marshmallows

5 tbsp (75 ml) whiskey

1 cup (240 g) prepared caramel sauce

1 cup (80 g) cooked bacon, crumbled

Line an 8 x 8-inch (20 x 20-cm) pan with parchment or wax paper, leaving a 1-inch (2.5-cm) overhang on each side.

Place the chocolate in the top of a double boiler or in a heatproof bowl above a pan of simmering water (make sure the water doesn't touch the bottom of the bowl). Heat on low until the chocolate is melted. Pour half of the melted chocolate into the parchment-lined pan. Using a spatula, spread the chocolate until smooth and even. Transfer the pan to the freezer and chill for about 5 minutes, or until the melted chocolate becomes solid. Keep the remaining chocolate warm.

Place the marshmallows in a large saucepan over medium to medium-low heat until they just start to melt and form web-like strands when stirred. Remove from the heat and add the whiskey. Stir to combine. Spread the marshmallow mixture over the solid chocolate layer.

Spread the caramel sauce on top of the marshmallow layer until smooth.

Transfer the pan to the freezer to chill for about 5 minutes, or until the caramel becomes slightly hardened. Pour the remaining half of the melted chocolate over the caramel layer and spread until smooth. Sprinkle and gently press the bacon crumbles into the chocolate. Return the fully assembled bark to the refrigerator to chill for 20 minutes, or until the bark becomes solid. Bring bark to room temperature before cutting.

MAPLE-BACON BREAD PUDDING

Here is another great recipe from my friend Nicole. Being from Maine, she knows a little something about maple syrup. I doubt this recipe will disappoint. Bacon, blueberries and maple syrup folded into warm egg- and cream-coated bread are a delight—I'm telling you, you will be licking your plate clean.

SERVES: APPROXIMATELY 8 • COOK TIME: APPROXIMATELY 1 HOUR

2 cups (400 g) sugar

5 large eggs

2 cups (480 ml) half-and-half

¼ cup (60 ml) dark amber maple syrup

¼ cup (35 g) dried blueberries (soaked in maple bourbon and drained, optional)

4 cups (200 g) crusty bread like Italian or French, crusts removed and cubed

¼ cup (56 g) butter, plus melted butter for coating the pan

1 cup (240 g) firmly packed brown sugar (light or dark)

2 cups (160 g) cooked bacon, any kind, crumbled

Bread Pudding Sauce, for serving (recipe follows)

½ gallon (1.8 L) vanilla ice cream

For this recipe, I like to use a non-insulated bullet-style cooker because it is such a short cook and I don't have to use a lot of cooking fuel. Preheat your smoker to 350°F (177°C).

In a large bowl, combine the sugar, eggs, half-and-half, syrup, blueberries and bread cubes.

Coat a 9 x 9-inch (23 x 23-cm) baking pan with melted butter.

Pour the custard and bread mixture into the baking pan, cover and refrigerate for at least 1 hour and up to overnight.

Combine the butter and brown sugar in a bowl and work with your fingers until crumbly. Top the bread and custard mixture with the brown sugar mixture.

Bake for 1 hour, until set. Top with the bacon crumbles and serve with the sauce and vanilla ice cream.

BREAD PUDDING SAUCE

1 cup (200 g) sugar

½ cup (112 g) butter

1 egg, beaten

2 tsp (10 ml) maple syrup

Combine all the ingredients in a small saucepan and cook over medium heat until the sugar melts, about 5 to 10 minutes.

BACON BLOODY MARY

Bloody Marys are a staple at any brunch, and rumor has it that it helps with the occasional hangover, or so I've heard (wink, wink). I like mine spicy and peppery—sometimes my hangovers end up that way, too. Here's a Bloody Mary recipe I think is a winner!

SERVES: 4 • PREP TIME: 15 MINUTES

8 strips Sriracha and Honey-Cured Pork Belly (page 23) or any bacon

6 cups (1440 ml) Bloody Mary mix, such as Ubons Bloody Mary Mix

Juice of ½ lemon

1 tbsp (15 ml) Worcestershire sauce

1 tsp (3 g) freshly cracked black pepper

1 tbsp (15 ml) hot sauce

¼–½ cup (60–120 g) prepared horseradish (I love horseradish, so I use ½ cup)

6 oz (180 ml) top-shelf vodka (I like Ketel One)

4 celery sticks

4 lemon wedges

Fire up your grill for indirect cooking. Simply light the charcoal using a charcoal chimney, and dump the hot coals into the grill. Stack the charcoal into a single pile on one side of the grill, and cook your food on the opposite side of the grill, away from the heat source.

Wrap 1 piece of bacon around each of 4 wooden skewers and cook on the indirect-heat zone until the bacon is browned, 15–20 minutes. Finely chop the remaining 4 pieces of bacon, cook and set aside.

In a large pitcher, combine the Bloody Mary mix, lemon juice, Worcestershire sauce, pepper, hot sauce and horseradish. Mix well and keep in the fridge until ready for use.

Fill 4 (16-ounce [480-ml]) glasses halfway with ice. Add equal amounts of the chopped bacon to each glass. Next, add 1½ ounces (45 ml) of vodka. Fill the glass with the Bloody Mary mix. Garnish each with a celery stick, lemon wedge and bacon swizzle stick, and enjoy. If you want it a little spicier, you can add a few more shakes of hot sauce.

CHAPTER 3

SAUSAGE, SAUSAGE AND MORE SAUSAGE

I still remember the first time my father and I cooked sausage over charcoal. We used a long silver fork with a black wooden handle to turn the sausage. He explained that sausage is wrapped in a casing, and that it would be better to use tongs instead of a fork, but we didn't have tongs handy. Needless to say, in my fledgling cooking adventure, I watched a sausage fall off the fork, slide between the grates of the hibachi grill and burn into a pile of ash. Yeah, now I usually make it a point to have tongs handy whenever I cook sausage. Some things you have to learn the hard way, and some memories are truly priceless.

Sausage is made from ground meat sprinkled with an assortment of herbs and spices, wrapped in a casing and cooked until sausagey-licious. Traditionally, the casing was made from animal intestine, but nowadays the casing is usually made from a very thin synthetic material that is edible. A food comprised largely of meat scraps that are ground into a mix, sausage variations are found across the globe. This versatile and tasty meat can be sliced, grilled, fried or simmered. Today, sausage is often made from pork butt, with a good ratio of fat to meat to help keep it moist and juicy. Some of my favorite variations on sausage are the more local varieties that I grew up with: mild Italian sausage, hot links, chourico and breakfast sausage. And of course, it goes without saying that no trip to Fenway Park would be complete without a visit to the sausage guy on Yawkey Way.

ITALIAN SAUSAGE (SWEET AND HOT)

In the United States, Italian sausage refers to a style of pork sausage that uses fennel as the primary seasoning. In Italy, people say that sausage goes back to Roman times. Italian sausage is primarily ground from pork butt and seasonings frequently include paprika, salt, black pepper, anise, oregano, thyme and garlic. In southern Italy, sausage usually contains fennel seeds, creating a slightly different flavor profile than what you'd find in most parts of the central and northern regions of the country.

In U.S. grocery stores, the two most common varieties of Italian sausage are hot and sweet (mild). The main difference between them is the addition of cayenne and more hot red pepper flakes.

Grinding your own meat to make sausage can be a lot of fun. Typically, I like to use a ratio of 75 percent meat and 25 percent fat. My favorite combination is 3 pounds (1.3 kg) of Boston butt and 1 pound (450 g) of pork belly. If you own a KitchenAid stand mixer, there is a meat grinder and sausage stuffer attachment. Not everyone has access to a meat grinder, though, so here I am going to show you how to make Italian sausage (without using a casing) just from ground pork found at your local market. If your local market doesn't have any ground pork readily available, just ask the meat person behind the counter and he or she will grind some up for you at no extra charge—all you need to do is ask.

SERVES: 8 • COOK TIME: 30 MINUTES • COOK TIME FOR GRILLING: 30 MINUTES

FOR THE SWEET SAUSAGE

2 lb (910 g) ground pork

1 tbsp (6 g) coarsely cracked black pepper

½ tsp white pepper

1 tbsp (1 g) dried parsley

2 tbsp (2 g) dried Italian seasoning mix

2 tbsp (12 g) minced garlic

¼ tsp red pepper flakes

2 tbsp (12 g) crushed dried fennel seed

1 tbsp (8 g) paprika

2 tbsp (20 g) minced onion

1 tbsp (18 g) kosher salt

1 tbsp (15 g) brown sugar (light or dark)

FOR THE HOT SAUSAGE

2 lb (910 g) ground pork

1 tbsp (6 g) coarsely cracked black pepper

½ tsp white pepper

1 tbsp (1 g) dried parsley

2 tbsp (2 g) dried Italian seasoning mix

2 tbsp (12 g) minced garlic

2 tbsp (10 g) red pepper flakes

2 tbsp (12 g) crushed dried fennel seed

2 tbsp (16 g) smoked paprika

1½ tsp (4 g) cayenne pepper

2 tbsp (20 g) minced onion

1 tbsp (18 g) kosher salt

(continued)

ITALIAN SAUSAGE (SWEET AND HOT) (CONTINUED)

You want to make sure the sausage meat is extremely cold (almost frozen) when you mix the ingredients together. You don't want the sausage meat to start warming up because the fat in the sausage will start to get soft, runny and smeary, which is not a good thing.

Choose which sausage you want to make (mild or hot) and mix all the ingredients together until well incorporated—you want to do this step quickly. Form into patties or links (without casings) and let them sit in the fridge for 1–2 hours before using, so the flavors all blend together. If you are not going to use right away, then freeze in ½ pound (228 g) portions.

Now, to cook these up, you can do a couple different things. You can either grill them over high heat or cook them low and slow in the smoker.

To grill them, set up your charcoal grill for two-zone cooking. Fill up a charcoal chimney with hardwood lump charcoal and light it. When flames start coming out of the top of the chimney, the coals are ready. Dump onto one side of the cooker. Keep the other side clear for indirect cooking.

Place the sausages on the direct-heat zone and cook for about 2 minutes, then turn them a quarter turn and cook for another 2 minutes, turn again a quarter turn and cook for 2 more minutes, and then turn one last time and cook for 2 minutes. Then move the sausage over to the indirect-heat zone to finish cooking for about 10–15 minutes, until you get an internal temperature of 160°F (71°C).

To smoke these sausages, fire up your smoker (I like to use my non-insulated bullet-style cooker) to 250°F (121°C) and add about ½ gallon (1.8 L) of hot water to the water pan. If your cooker doesn't have a water pan, simply fill up a disposable aluminum pan and place it in the bottom of the smoker. Place the sausage on the top cooking grate. Add 2 chunks of smoke wood (apple or sugar maple) and cook for 1–1½ hours, until you reach an internal temperature of 160°F (71°C).

Chunks of pork being stuffed into meat grinder attachment to make sausage.

ANDOUILLE SAUSAGE

Heavily seasoned, and typically smoked using pecan, hickory or sugar cane, andouille sausage is part of many Cajun dishes in the Louisiana bayou. While cayenne or red pepper flakes, black pepper and garlic are common ingredients, some recipes rely on a wider palate of flavors, such as thyme, cloves, paprika and allspice, to obtain the sausage's bold and assertive flavors. For this recipe, it would be best to grind your own meat to make the sausage.

SERVES: APPROXIMATELY 12 • COOK TIME: APPROXIMATELY 1–2 HOURS

3 lb (1.4 kg) pork butt

1 lb (455 g) pork belly

4 tbsp (32 g) paprika

1 tbsp (8 g) coarsely ground black pepper

1 tbsp (8 g) ground cumin

1 tbsp (8 g) cayenne pepper

1 tbsp (18 g) kosher salt

1 tsp (2 g) red pepper flakes

1 tsp (2 g) dried oregano

1 tsp (2 g) dried thyme

1 tsp (2 g) ground coriander

¼ cup (40 g) minced onion

¼ cup (24 g) minced garlic

Sausage casings (optional)

Cut the pork butt and pork belly into 1-inch (2.5-cm) cubes and place in a large bowl. Add the remaining ingredients and mix well. Cover with plastic wrap and refrigerate for up to 24 hours.

Grind the meat, using a large die, into a chilled stainless steel bowl. You want to make sure the sausage meat is extremely cold (almost frozen). You don't want the sausage meat to start warming up because the fat in the sausage will start to get soft, runny and smeary, which is not a good thing.

Try to work as quickly as you can. If you have to, grind the sausage in small batches, such as 1 or 2 pound (455 or 910 g) portions. By keeping the meat very cold, it helps with the grinding process and it's also a good idea from a food safety standpoint.

From here, you can either stuff the sausage into casings or make free-form patties; it's your choice.

Now you're ready to smoke these bad boys up. For this recipe, I like to use an insulated cabinet smoker, and fire it up to 250°F (121°C). If you are using an uninsulated bullet-style cooker (like a WSM), pay attention to the water pan to make sure it doesn't run out of water and cook on the top cooking grate. Cook the sausages for 1–2 hours. If you're going to eat the sausages right away, cook them to an internal temperature of 160°F (71°C). However, if you're planning to use them another time, such as in another recipe, you should only cook them to an internal temperature of 150°F (66°C). That way, you still have some room to work with the sausage when you heat it up the next time around. Sausage will keep in the freezer for several months or in your refrigerator for a few days.

NOTE: If you want to make sausage links, I recommend asking your local butcher for natural casings. Other places, such as Cabela's and Bass Pro Shops, sell artificial casings. To use the casings, tie one end into a knot. If you're using your KitchenAid sausage stuffer attachment, spray the tube with nonstick cooking spray, and slide the casing onto the lubricated surface until you get to where the knot is tied. Hold the casing loosely in one hand and let the sausage fill the casing as you feed it through the stuffer.

BREAKFAST SAUSAGE

Who doesn't love some breakfast sausage in the morning, fried up with some eggs and home fries? What about sausage gravy with fresh, homemade biscuits? I'm going to show you how to make three different kinds of breakfast sausage (yes, three kinds): savory, hot (spicy) and maple (sweet). There is a good chance that these recipes are going to change the way you think about breakfast! You can get the meat from the butcher or grind your own (see page 81).

SERVES: 4 • COOK TIME: 20 MINUTES

FOR THE SAVORY SAUSAGE

1 lb (455 g) ground pork

1 tsp (6 g) salt

¼ tsp garlic salt

½ tsp dried parsley

¾ tsp ground sage

¼ tsp coarsely ground black pepper

¼ tsp dried thyme

¼ tsp red pepper flakes

¼ tsp ground coriander

⅛ tsp dried oregano

FOR THE HOT SAUSAGE

1 lb (455 g) ground pork

1 tsp (6 g) salt

½ tsp cayenne pepper (or more, depending on how hot you want it)

¼ tsp rubbed sage

¼ tsp coarsely ground black pepper

¼ tsp red pepper flakes

¼ tsp ground coriander

FOR THE MAPLE (SWEET) SAUSAGE

1 lb (455 g) ground pork

3 tbsp (45 ml) maple syrup

1 tsp (6 g) salt

½ tsp MSG (optional)

¼ tsp ground coriander

¼ tsp black pepper

You want to make sure the sausage meat is extremely cold (almost frozen) when you mix the ingredients together. You don't want the sausage meat to start warming up because the fat in the sausage will start to get soft, runny and smeary, which is not a good thing.

Once you have your sausage mixed, then form into sausage logs or patties. Store the sausage in the fridge until ready to cook.

To grill them, set up your charcoal grill for two-zone cooking. Fill up a charcoal chimney with hardwood lump charcoal and light it. When flames start coming out of the top of the chimney, the coals are ready. Dump onto one side of the cooker. Keep the other side clear for indirect cooking.

Place the sausages on the direct-heat zone and cook for about 2 minutes, then turn them a quarter turn and cook for another 2 minutes, again a quarter turn and cook for 2 more minutes, and one last time a quarter turn and cook for 2 minutes. Then move the sausages over to the indirect-heat zone to finish cooking for about 10–15 minutes, until you get an internal temperature of 160°F (71°C).

To smoke these sausages, fire up your smoker to 250°F (121°C). For this recipe, I like to use my non-insulated bullet-style cooker with about ½ gallon (1.8 L) of hot water in the water pan. If your cooker doesn't have a water pan, simply fill up a disposable aluminum pan and place it in the bottom of the smoker. Place the sausage on the top cooking grate. Add 2 chunks of your smoke wood (apple or sugar maple) and cook for 1–1½ hours, until you reach an internal temperature of 160°F (71°C).

CHOURICO SAUSAGE

Indigenous to the Iberian Peninsula, these sausages are often made from a mix of pork belly, pork shoulder and beef. While they're typically seasoned with salt, white pepper, oregano, cayenne and pimento, it is paprika (dried smoked red pepper) that provides the deep hue so often associated with these links. The Latin American variant uses chili peppers, which tend to bring a little more heat to the table. All you need is a simple sausage grinder that you can get at most department stores.

SERVES: APPROXIMATELY 12 • COOK TIME: APPROXIMATELY 1–2 HOURS

3 lb (1.4 kg) pork shoulder or butt

1 lb (455 g) pork belly

3 tbsp (24 g) sweet smoked paprika

⅓ cup (45 g) hot smoked paprika

6 cloves garlic, finely chopped

1½ tbsp (27 g) kosher salt

1½ tsp (3 g) fennel seeds

1 tsp (3 g) cayenne pepper

¾ cup (180 ml) red wine

2 tsp (6 g) ground black pepper

Sausage casings (optional)

Cut the pork shoulder or butt and pork belly in 1-inch (2.5-cm) cubes and place into a large bowl. Add the remaining ingredients and mix well. Cover with plastic wrap and refrigerate for up to 24 hours.

Grind the meat, using a large die, into a chilled stainless steel bowl. You want to make sure the sausage meat is extremely cold (almost frozen). You don't want the sausage meat to start warming up because the fat in the sausage will start to get soft, runny and smeary, which is not a good thing.

Try to work as quickly as you can. If you have to, grind the sausage in small batches, such as 1 or 2 pound (455 or 910 g) portions. By keeping the meat very cold, it helps with the grinding process and it's also a good idea from a food safety standpoint.

From here, you can either stuff the sausage into casings or make free-form patties; it's your choice.

Now you're ready to smoke these bad boys up. For this recipe, I like to use an insulated cabinet smoker, and fire it up to 250°F (121°C). If you are using an uninsulated bullet-style cooker (like a WSM), pay attention to the water pan to make sure it doesn't run out of water and cook on the top cooking grate. Cook the sausages for 1–2 hours. If you're going to eat the sausages right away, cook them to an internal temperature of 160°F (71°C). However, if you're planning to use them another time, such as in another recipe, you should only cook them to an internal temperature of 150°F (66°C). That way, you still have some room to work with the sausage when you heat it up the next time around. Sausage will keep in the freezer for several months or in your refrigerator for a few days.

CHEDDAR JALAPEÑO BRATWURST

The name *bratwurst* most often refers to a sausage made from pork in a natural casing that is grilled or fried in a pan. It is a favorite in Germany, with each region having its own specialty.

More than fifty kinds of bratwurst are available in Germany, differing in size, seasonings and texture. This recipe is going to make about 5 pounds (2.3 kg) of the best bratwurst you have ever had! Why? Because homemade is always better than store-bought! All you need is a simple sausage grinder that you can get at most department stores. This recipe is perfect for your next summer cookout or party, or any other time of the year.

SERVES: 10 • COOK TIME FOR SMOKING: APPROXIMATELY 2 HOURS • COOK TIME FOR GRILLING: APPROXIMATELY 30 MINUTES

3¾ lb (1.7 kg) ground pork butt

1¼ lb (568 g) pork belly

2 eggs

1 cup (240 ml) beer (I like Samuel Adams Boston Lager)

½ cup (68 g) minced jalapeños

8 oz (225 g) shredded cheddar cheese

1½ tsp (4 g) black pepper

1 tsp (3 g) cayenne pepper

1 tsp (3 g) paprika (I use smoked)

½ tsp ground nutmeg

1 tbsp (8 g) dry mustard

1 tbsp (8 g) ground coriander

1 tsp (2 g) ground sage

5 tsp (30 g) kosher salt

2 tsp (8 g) sugar

2 tsp (5 g) onion powder

2–3 chunks apple wood (optional)

Cut the pork into 1-inch (2.5-cm) cubes and grind through a ¼-inch (6-mm) grinding plate. (Or you can pulse with a food processor in small batches.)

In a medium-size mixing bowl, beat together the eggs and beer until well blended. Add the jalapeños, cheese and all the seasonings. In a large bowl, combine the ground meat and wet mixture until well incorporated.

Cover with plastic wrap and refrigerate from 2 to 24 hours, the longer the better.

Grind the meat, using a large die, into a chilled stainless steel bowl. You want to make sure the sausage meat is extremely cold (almost frozen). You don't want the sausage meat to start warming up because the fat in the sausage will start to get soft, runny and smeary, which is not a good thing.

Try to work as quickly as you can. If you have to, grind the sausage in small batches, such as 1 or 2 pound (455 or 910 g) portions. By keeping the meat very cold, it helps with the grinding process and it's also a good idea from a food safety standpoint.

At this point, you can stuff the sausage into casings (see page 83), wrap it in 1-pound (455-g) packages and freeze for a few months, or bring it out to your smoker/grill and cook it up (that's what I like to do because I can't wait to eat it!).

Now, there are two ways you can cook these sausages: on the smoker or on the grill. I will show you both ways.

SETUP FOR YOUR SMOKER

Fire up your smoker and let the cooking temperature stabilize at 225°F–250°F (107°C–121°C). I like to use 2 or 3 fist-size chunks of apple wood. Place the brats in the smoker, and add the smoke wood. Cook for about 2 hours, until the internal temperature is over 160°F (71°C).

(continued)

CHEDDAR JALAPEÑO BRATWURST (CONTINUED)

SETUP FOR YOUR GRILL

Set up your charcoal grill to two-zone cooking. Fill up a charcoal chimney with hardwood lump charcoal and light it. When flames start coming out of the top of the chimney, the coals are ready. Dump onto one side of the cooker. Keep the other side clear for indirect cooking.

Place the brats on the grill grate over the direct-heat zone. Put the cover on the grill and let cook for about 2 minutes. Flip the brats over and cook another 2 minutes. Move the brats to the indirect-heat zone of the grill for the rest of the cook. Continue cooking until you reach an internal temperature of 160°F (71°C), about 30 minutes.

CHOURICO AND CORNBREAD STUFFING

One year for Thanksgiving, I wanted to try my hand at making stuffing. I messed around in the kitchen, and after a couple of attempts, I came up with this recipe. What's not to love about cornbread and chourico? The spices of the chourico and the sweetness of the cornbread were a perfect match in my mind. Every year, my sister asks if I'm going to make my cornbread stuffing, so my family now has two different types of stuffing to pick from at holiday gatherings!

SERVES: APPROXIMATELY 6 • COOK TIME: APPROXIMATELY 1 HOUR

2 tbsp (30 ml) olive oil

½ cup (75 g) fresh corn kernels

1 Granny Smith apple, cored, peeled and diced

1 shallot, diced

1 clove garlic, minced

6 cups (600 g) cubed and toasted cornbread

1 lb (455 g) Chourico Sausage (page 86), cooked and diced into ¼" (6-mm) pieces

4 tbsp (56 g) melted unsalted butter

2 cups (480 ml) chicken stock, heated

Salt and pepper

The cooking temperature for this recipe is 375°F (190°C). I like to use my non-insulated bullet-style smoker for this recipe because I can get it up to temperature rather quickly, and this is a relatively short cook.

In a small frying pan on the stove top, heat the olive oil and sauté the corn, apples, shallot and garlic for 10-15 minutes until golden. Set aside until ready to use.

Pour the cornbread into a half-size disposable aluminum pan, add the sautéed veggies and chourico sausage and mix well. Add the melted butter and heated chicken stock. Mix until well incorporated. Season with salt and pepper to taste. Cover with heavy-duty foil, place on the top rack of the cooker and cook for 30-40 minutes. Uncover and cook an additional 20 minutes, until the top gets a little crunchy and crusty.

SAUSAGE CACCIATORE

Cacciatore means "hunter" in Italian, and so a *cacciatore* refers to a meal prepared "hunter style," with tomatoes, onions, herbs, often bell pepper and sometimes wine. Cacciatore is usually made with braised chicken, but I am substituting sausage.

SERVES: 4 • COOK TIME: APPROXIMATELY 3 HOURS

2 lb (910 g) Hot or Sweet Italian Sausage (page 81) (about 8 links)

¼ cup (60 ml) olive oil

1 medium sweet onion, thinly sliced

1 green bell pepper, cored and thinly sliced

1 red bell pepper, cored and thinly sliced

1 cup (70 g) sliced baby portobello mushrooms

3 cloves garlic, minced

Salt and pepper

½ cup (120 ml) red wine (merlot or cabernet)

2 (28-oz [784-g]) cans whole peeled tomatoes with basil (I use Tuttorosso brand)

1 tbsp (1 g) dried oregano

2 tbsp (2.5 g) chopped fresh basil

1 lb (455 g) linguini, cooked according to package directions

This recipe is going to be made in a Dutch oven over a charcoal grill. Fire up your charcoal grill for two-zone cooking. Fill up a charcoal chimney with hardwood lump charcoal and light it. When flames start coming out of the top of the chimney, the coals are ready. Dump onto one side of the cooker. Keep the other side clear for indirect cooking.

Once the coals are ready, place the sausage on the grill grates for direct-heat grilling. Cook for 2–3 minutes, then flip and cook an additional 2–3 minutes. Remove from the grill and set aside.

Place the Dutch oven on the cooking grate over the direct-heat zone. Pour the olive oil into the Dutch oven and let it heat up. Stir in the onion, peppers, mushrooms and garlic. Season with salt and pepper, and cook until the onions are translucent, 5–7 minutes. Add the red wine and cook 5 more minutes. Add the tomatoes, oregano, basil and the cooked whole sausages. Cover the Dutch oven and move it to the indirect side of the grill; cook for 1½ hours. Rotate the Dutch oven 180 degrees and cook for 1 more hour. Remember, the sausage is finished cooking once it obtains an internal temperature of 160°F (71°C). The rest of the cooking time is simply to help the flavors of the dish meld together. Remove from the heat and serve over the linguini.

BUFFALO CHICKEN-STUFFED SAUSAGE FATTY

I am always looking for new ways to use sausage, and a new filling for a sausage fatty is one of those ways! A fatty is ground sausage formed into a log (think Jimmy Dean sausage). The log can be seasoned or stuffed with your favorite ingredients, and is often wrapped in bacon. Not too long ago, I decided to try making one with Buffalo chicken inside. I love Buffalo chicken, so I figured, why not? The only thing I regret is that I didn't think to try this sooner! Don't make the same mistake I made—get the smoker going and cross this off your to-do list!

SERVES: 8 • COOK TIME: APPROXIMATELY 2½ HOURS

1 lb (455 g) Hot Breakfast Sausage (page 84) or Jimmy Dean breakfast sausage

1 lb (455 g) Sweet Italian Sausage (page 81) or ground sweet Italian sausage

½ lb (225 g) Chourico Sausage (page 86) or ground chourico sausage

½ lb (225 g) chicken, cooked and cut into ½" (1.3-cm) cubes

½ cup (60 g) blue cheese crumbles

1 cup (120 g) shredded cheddar cheese

¼ cup (25 g) chopped green onion

1½ cups (355 ml) Buffalo Sauce (page 178)

¼–½ cup (32-64 g) Smokin' Hoggz All-Purpose Rub (page 181)

In a large bowl, combine all the sausage mixes, place in a gallon (3.8 L) plastic bag, and flatten out until the mixture reaches all sides of the bag and is of equal thickness throughout (about ½-inch [1.3-cm] thick). Spray a sheet of aluminum foil with nonstick cooking spray. Remove the mixture from the bag and place on the sheet of aluminum foil (an easy way to do this is to simply cut the bag open).

In a separate bowl, combine the cooked chicken, blue cheese, cheddar cheese, green onion and Buffalo sauce to taste: if you like it spicy, use 1 cup (240 ml); if not, use ½ cup (120 ml). Take the chicken mixture and place in the center of the sausage mixture. Roll the entire thing into a log and completely season the outside with the rub.

Fire up a grill or smoker to 275°F (135°C). Place the sausage fatty on the grate and cook for 2-2½ hours, or until the internal temperature reaches 160°F (71°C). You can add any kind of smoke wood you like. (I like apple or sugar maple.) During the last 30 minutes, brush on the remaining Buffalo Sauce.

Take the fatty off the cooker and let rest for about 1 hour. Slice into 1-1½-inch (2.5-3.8-cm) slices. Serve with blue cheese dressing and celery and carrot sticks. Football games will never be the same again.

PHILLY CHEESESTEAK SAUSAGE FATTY

I finally had my first real cheesesteak about two years ago at a barbecue contest just outside of Philly. My friends from Pigheaded BBQ hooked us up! Now, I've had steak-and-cheese sandwiches before, but nothing compares to an authentic Philly cheesesteak! The key is using the best steak you can possibly get. I'm not talking about the shaved stuff you get in the supermarket—I'm talking thinly cut (about ⅛-inch [3-mm] thick) rib eye steak. And, of course, American cheese. Here's my take on a Philly cheesesteak, with a little twist—it's wrapped in sausage!

SERVES: 8 • COOK TIME: APPROXIMATELY 2½ HOURS

1½ lb (680 g) Breakfast Sausage (page 84)

1½ lb (680 g) Sweet Italian Sausage (page 81)

1 lb (455 g) thinly shaved rib eye steak, cooked

½ sweet onion, sliced about ¼" (6-mm) thick, cooked

8 slices American deli cheese

1 cup (120 g) Cheez Whiz

Salt and pepper

½ cup (120 g) ketchup, plus more for serving

In a large bowl, combine both the sausage mixes, place in a gallon (3.8 L) plastic bag, and flatten out until the mixture reaches all sides of the bag and is of equal thickness throughout (about ½-inch [1.3-cm] thick). Spray a sheet of aluminum foil with nonstick cooking spray. Remove the mixture from the bag and place on the sheet of aluminum foil (an easy way to do this is to simply cut the bag open).

Place the steak and onion in the center of the sausage. Top with the American cheese and Cheez Whiz and roll the entire thing into a log. Completely season the outside with salt and pepper.

Fire up a grill or smoker to 275°F (135°C). Place the sausage fatty on the grate and cook for 2–2½ hours, or until the internal temperature reaches 160°F (71°C). You can add any kind of smoke wood you like. (I like apple or sugar maple.) During the last 30 minutes, brush on the ketchup.

Take the fatty off the cooker and let rest for about 1 hour. Slice into 1–1½-inch (2.5–3.8-cm) slices and serve with more ketchup. That's right, I said *ketchup!* Trust me on this one!

KIELBASA SANDWICH WITH SWEET GRILLED ONIONS AND SAUERKRAUT

My wife came up with this recipe at a grilling contest we had entered. The category was kielbasa and we placed second. Let me tell you, the way that the sweet onions balance the jalapeño jelly makes this sandwich ridiculously delicious. This has become one of my favorite sandwiches to eat and is now a consistent staple in our meal planning.

SERVES: 8 • COOK TIME: 15 MINUTES

½ cup (90 g) whole-grain mustard

½ cup (90 g) Dijon mustard

½ cup (120 g) spicy jalapeño jelly

1 lb (455 g) kielbasa, sliced into ¼" (6-mm) circles

1 large sweet onion, sliced into thin rounds

12 oz (336 g) sauerkraut

8 oz (225 g) Gruyère cheese

8 small crusty rolls

In a small bowl, mix together the mustards and jelly until well combined.

Fire up a charcoal grill, heat up a cast-iron skillet and brown the kielbasa. Once it is slightly darkened around edges, remove it from the pan and set aside.

In the same pan, add the sweet onions and grill until they just begin to brown and soften. Add the sauerkraut to the pan with the onions and cook together until the juices evaporate, about 8 minutes. Transfer to a bowl and set aside.

Using the same cast-iron skillet, create 4 piles of the kielbasa rounds (6–8 in each pile). Add the onion and sauerkraut mixture, then top with a good slice of Gruyère cheese. Cover the cast-iron skillet with aluminum foil and let the cheese melt.

While the cheese is melting, slice your rolls. Depending on the roll, I like to scoop out a bit of the inside bread so the sandwich is not too bready.

Assemble the sandwiches. Spread some of the mustard and jelly condiment on the bottom bun. Place the pile of kielbasa rounds with the onions, sauerkraut and cheese mixture on top. Top off with the roll. Repeat to make 7 more sandwiches. Then serve—simple and delicious!

CHOURICO AND MUSSELS

This is one of my favorite sausage and seafood dishes. If we go out to a restaurant and this dish is on the menu, I almost always order it—I absolutely love this dish! The best part is the broth at the end, so make sure you have some nice crusty bread to sop up that savory broth.

SERVES: 4 • COOK TIME: APPROXIMATELY 20 MINUTES

2 tbsp (30 ml) extra virgin olive oil

1 sweet onion, sliced ¼" (6-mm) thick

½ tsp red pepper flakes

Kosher salt

4 links Chourico Sausage (page 86), sliced ½" (1.3-cm) thick

3 cloves garlic, thinly sliced

1 cup (240 ml) white wine

1 cup (240 ml) chicken stock

8 canned plum tomatoes, quartered

4 dozen mussels

8 pieces crusty bread (I like French bread for this)

This recipe will be made on a charcoal grill. Set up your grill for two-zone cooking. Fill up a charcoal chimney with hardwood lump charcoal and light it. When flames start coming out of the top of the chimney, the coals are ready. Dump onto one side of the cooker. Keep the other side clear for indirect cooking.

Place a cast-iron pan on the direct-heat zone. Add the olive oil. Add the onion, red pepper flakes and about 1 teaspoon (5 g) of kosher salt. Sauté until the onions are translucent, about 6 minutes. Add the chourico and garlic and sauté for another 3–4 minutes. Add the white wine, chicken stock, tomatoes and mussels. Cover the pan with heavy-duty foil and bring to a boil. Steam until the mussels open, about 5 minutes. You may need to move the pan to the indirect-heat zone if it starts to boil over.

Divide the chourico and mussels evenly among 4 large soup bowls, discarding any mussels that did not open. Pour the broth over the mussels. Serve with the crusty French bread, and prepare to say, "Yum!"

CHOURICO AND PEPPER PORTUGUESE SANDWICHES

I have a friend who is 100 percent Portuguese and any time we would get together to watch a sporting event, he would always make this dish. He would use ground chourico and would serve it on Portuguese sweet rolls, kind of like a sloppy joe, but unbelievably better! In this recipe, I am going to use chunks of chourico and ground chourico to give the sandwich a little more texture. I'll also cook using the smoker to create a little more flavor.

SERVES: 8–12 • COOK TIME: APPROXIMATELY 3 HOURS

1 lb (455 g) ground Chourico Sausage (page 86)

1 lb (455 g) Chourico Sausage (page 86), cut into ½" (1.3-cm) chunks

2–3 chunks cherry wood

2 tbsp (30 ml) olive oil

2 onions, diced

2 green bell peppers, cored and diced

1 (14-oz [392-g]) can diced tomatoes, with liquid

1 (8-oz [225-g]) can tomato paste

¾ cup (180 ml) red wine

Salt

8–12 Portuguese sweet rolls

For this recipe, I like to use an insulated cabinet smoker. Fire up the smoker and let the cooking temperature stabilize at 250°F–275°F (121°C–135°C). If you are using an uninsulated bullet-style cooker (like a WSM), pay attention to the water pan to make sure it doesn't run out of water and cook on the top cooking grate.

What I like to do is get a little bit of smoke on the sausage before the whole sandwich comes together. Add the cherry wood just before you add the food to the smoker. Place all the sausage in the smoker for about 1 hour. Remove the sausage.

Place the olive oil in a medium frying pan. Brown the onions and peppers for about 5 minutes.

Combine the sausage, onions, peppers, tomatoes with their liquid, tomato paste, wine and salt to taste in a half-size disposable aluminum pan. Place the uncovered pan into the smoker for about 2 hours. Stir well and then cover with heavy-duty aluminum foil. Cook for another hour. Remove from the smoker and let it sit for 30–45 minutes.

Serve on the Portuguese sweet rolls.

JAMBALAYA WITH ANDOUILLE SAUSAGE, SHRIMP AND CHICKEN

Every year we host a Super Bowl party, and this dish is a staple for the event. It wouldn't be the Super Bowl if we didn't have jambalaya. It's spicy, savory and stick-to-your ribs delicious!

SERVES: APPROXIMATELY 8–12 PEOPLE • COOK TIME: APPROXIMATELY 2 HOURS

FOR THE CREOLE SEASONING

2½ tbsp (20 g) paprika

1 tbsp (18 g) salt

1 tbsp (8 g) black pepper

1 tbsp (8 g) chili powder

½ tbsp (4 g) cayenne pepper

1 tbsp (1 g) dried oregano

1 tbsp (1 g) dried thyme

¼ cup (60 ml) olive oil

1 large onion, diced

1 green bell pepper, cored and diced

1 red bell pepper, cored and diced

4 cloves garlic, minced

1 (28-oz [784-g]) can whole peeled tomatoes, quartered, liquid reserved

1 (8-oz [225-g]) can tomato paste

1 qt (940 ml) low-sodium chicken stock

1½ cups (240 g) uncooked rice

2 lb (910 g) Andouille Sausage (page 83), cut into ½" (1.3-cm) rounds, or use store-bought

2 lb (910 g) shrimp (extra-large), peeled, deveined and cut in half

1 lb (455 g) grilled chicken, cut into ½" (1.3-cm) cubes

First, make the Creole Seasoning by combining all the ingredients in a small bowl and store in a jar with a tight-fitting lid.

This recipe will be made using a charcoal grill and a large Dutch oven. Fire up your grill for two-zone cooking. Fill up a charcoal chimney with hardwood lump charcoal and light it. When flames start coming out of the top of the chimney, the coals are ready. Dump onto one side of the cooker. Keep the other side clear for indirect cooking.

Place a Dutch oven on the cooking grate over the coals to heat up. Add the olive oil, and then add the onion, peppers and garlic. Sauté until the onions become translucent, about 5 minutes. Next, add the tomatoes, tomato paste and ½ cup (65 g) of the Creole Seasoning. Stir until the tomato paste is mixed in. Let cook for about 10 minutes. If the jambalaya starts to get too hot, move the Dutch oven over to the indirect-heat zone for a couple of minutes. After it cools for a few moments, move it back to the direct-heat zone and continue cooking.

Add the chicken stock and return to a boil. Then add the rice. Cover the Dutch oven and move to the indirect-heat zone. Place the lid on the grill, and let the rice cook for about 15 minutes. Finally, add the sausage, shrimp and chicken. Continue cooking on the indirect-heat side of the grill until the shrimp are cooked and the rice is soft, about 30 more minutes. Serve and enjoy the game!

CHAPTER 4

RIBS, CHOPS AND LOINS

With the exception of bacon, ribs might be my favorite part of the pig to turn into something delicious. My desire to learn how to make a tasty and tender rack of ribs is the main reason I became interested in competition barbecue. I've spent several years and many, many long hours trying to perfect a process for making great ribs.

One really fun thing about ribs is that they're so messy to eat. Another is the abundant variety. Throughout the country, you'll find rib variations that use a dry rub, a sweet sauce, a peppery tomato and vinegar sauce or a mustard sauce. You'll also find that some people select spareribs, while others prefer baby back ribs.

When people talk about spareribs, they're usually referring to the larger section of the rib cage located above the pig's sternum area. Spareribs tend to be flatter than baby back ribs, and while they usually contain more meat, spareribs also have more fat content. The fat renders during the cooking process, creating what many people describe as a more tender rib.

Baby back ribs are from the upper region of the rib bone that connects to the pork loin. Also known as loin back ribs, they tend to be shorter and more curved than spareribs. I actually think the meat on a baby back rib is a little bit sweeter than your typical sparerib.

Although I don't think any other meat provides quite the same dining experience as eating ribs, I'm also a fan of a good pork chop. Ribs, loins and chops come from regions of the animal that are adjacent to one another. In fact, a pork chop is the loin muscle with part of the baby back bone still connected to it. Pork chops are cut perpendicular to the spine, giving them their shape.

Now it's time for something a little bit more confusing: pork loin. For starters, the loin is not the same muscle as the tenderloin. Yeah, I sort of know what you're thinking. I was just as confused the first time I learned it, too. Pork loin is a long, thick and lean muscle taken from the animal's back. Because pork loin is lean, it's usually cooked over moderate heat or seared and then roasted. On the other hand, pork tenderloin is a small, tender muscle that runs right against the pig's backbone. The tenderloin is a delicate muscle that cooks quickly and easily dries out if you're not careful. Don't worry, though, you strike me as one of the careful types.

Pork is a versatile meat, and just about any cut will lend itself well to brining, marinating or smoking. Now, are you ready to try some?

COMPETITION RIBS

Ribs are what led me to my obsession with competition barbecue. I started using Saint Louis–style ribs at competitions because they are meatier and have a little bit more fat content than the more common baby back ribs. When cooked properly, spareribs are juicy, tender and oh, so flavorful. Our competition team has won New England Barbecue Society Ribs Team of the Year for three years in a row! This recipe has been tweaked a little bit from the one used in my last cookbook, so I wanted to share the new one with you.

SERVES: APPROXIMATELY 16 • COOK TIME: 4–4½ HOURS

1 cup (240 ml) Smokin' Hoggz Barbecue Sauce or Honey BBQ Sauce (page 173)

1 cup (240 ml) barbecue sauce, such as original flavor Head Country Bar-B-Q Sauce

4 racks Saint Louis-cut spareribs

1 cup (128 g) spicy dry rub, such as Smokin' Guns Hot Rub

1 cup (128 g) mild dry rub, such as Smokin' Guns Sweet Heat Rub

2 chunks sugar maple wood

2 chunks apple wood

16 oz (910 g) honey, divided

2 cups (480 g) firmly packed brown sugar (light or dark), divided

4 tsp (9 g) onion powder, divided

½ cup (112 g) butter, divided

In a small bowl, mix the barbecue sauces together and set aside until ready to use.

For this recipe, I like to use an insulated cabinet smoker. Set up your smoker for low and slow cooking at 250°F (121°C). If you are using an uninsulated bullet-style cooker (like a WSM), pay attention to the water pan and your fuel to make sure it doesn't run out of water or fuel and cook on the top cooking grate.

Lay out the racks of ribs with the meat side facing down. Apply ½ cup (64 g) of each rub to the back of the ribs, and let the rub set up for about 10 minutes. Flip the ribs over and apply the remaining ½ cup (64 g) of the rubs to the meat side. Let the ribs sit for about 30 minutes to allow the rub to set up.

Depending on which cooker you are using, you may not be able to fit all 4 racks on one cooking grate. If this is the case, place 2 racks on one grate and 2 on another grate for more balanced heat flow. Add the sugar maple wood and apple wood just prior to putting the ribs on the smoker. Place the ribs in the smoker and cook for about 1½ hours, then switch the ribs from the top rack to the bottom rack and vice versa (if needed). Continue cooking for another 1½ hours.

Lay out 4 sheets of heavy-duty foil. On each piece of foil, create layers by pouring ¼ cup (80 g) of the honey, sprinkling ¼ cup (60 g) of the brown sugar and ½ teaspoon of the onion powder on the honey layer, and then adding 2 tablespoons (28 g) of the butter on the sugar and powder layer. Lay the ribs, meat side down, on top of the layered ingredients. To each rack of ribs, apply ¼ cup (80 g) of the honey, ¼ cup (60 g) of the brown sugar, ½ teaspoon of the onion powder, and ¼ cup (60 ml) of the barbecue sauce mixture on top of the ribs and wrap tightly.

Return the ribs to the smoker. Let them cook for about 1 hour, then check the ribs for doneness. To check if ribs are done, unwrap one rack and look at the back side of the ribs. First, the meat will have shrunk from the bone ¼–½ inch (6–13 mm). Second, the bones will start to pop through on the back side.

If the ribs are done, remove them from the smoker. Open the foil and let the ribs vent for about 10 minutes. This is important because it will stop them from cooking any further.

Combine about ½ cup (120 ml) of juices from the foil and ½ cup (120 ml) of the barbecue sauce mixture and brush this on the ribs as a glaze. Cut the ribs and serve.

(continued)

Separating breast bone to make St. Louis cut.

Removing excess fat.

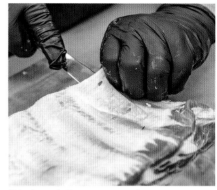
Using butter knife to remove membrane.

Peeling membrane.

Continuing to peel membrane.

Seasoning St. Louis–trimmed ribs.

COMPETITION RIBS (CONTINUED)

SAINT LOUIS–STYLE RIBS

You can trim full spareribs down to Saint Louis style in four easy steps. When you have a full rack of spareribs, it comes with the breastbone still attached; this has a lot of cartilage, which in my opinion is not too pleasant to eat, but the meat around it is still good, so don't throw it away.

The first thing you want to do is remove the flap, which is located at the narrow end of the rack (next to the last bone) and will overcook if not removed. To remove it, make a vertical cut about ½-inch (1.3-cm) from the last bone.

Next, you want to remove the breastbone and cartilage. To do that, find the longest bone, usually the third or fourth bone in from the wider side of the rack. Feel along that bone until you get to the knuckle—that's the start of the cartilage. From that point, cut by inserting the knife into the soft spot, then slicing perpendicular to the ribs, cutting through all of the soft spots where each rib meets the breastbone. Once the breastbone is removed, you should have a clean, rectangular rack of ribs. At this point you have a Saint Louis–style rack of ribs and they can be cooked, but I like to do two more things before I cook my ribs.

Flip the ribs over and remove the piece of skirt meat that runs the length of the rack.

Finally, I like to remove the membrane; this will translate into a better rib-eating experience, trust me. Once cooked, the membrane will turn to a paperlike consistency and no one wants to eat paper! You are now ready to cook your Saint Louis–style ribs!

SIMPLE SPICED PORK LOIN

This pork loin recipe is a very simple to make and you can use the end result for just about anything—from making roast pork sandwiches to having pork loin with gravy on top served with mashed potatoes and veggies. You may be thinking, "Well, why is this recipe in the cookbook then?" Because I am going to show you how to cook a pork loin so it comes out tender, juicy and absolutely perfect each and every time.

SERVES: APPROXIMATELY 10–12 • COOK TIME: APPROXIMATELY 2–3 HOURS

4 tbsp (72 g) salt

1 tbsp (8 g) pepper

2 tsp (4 g) garlic powder

2 tsp (6 g) chili powder

1 (5-lb [2.3-kg]) pork loin

Olive oil

3-4 chunks apple wood or peach wood

In a small bowl, combine the salt, pepper, garlic powder and chili powder and store in an airtight container until ready to use.

For this recipe, I like to use my insulated cabinet smoker, and will fire it up to about 225°F (107°C). Fill the water pan with about 1 gallon (3.8 L) of hot tap water. If your cooker doesn't have a water pan, simply fill up a disposable aluminum pan and place it in the bottom of the smoker. If you are using an uninsulated bullet-style cooker (like a WSM), pay attention to the water pan and your fuel to make sure it doesn't run out of water or fuel and cook on the top cooking grate.

While you are waiting for the cooker to come up to temperature, take the pork loin out of the fridge. Drizzle it with olive oil, making sure the entire loin is coated. Next, take the dry seasoning mix and liberally cover the entire pork loin. Let the loin sit at room temperature for 30 minutes.

When the cooker gets up to temperature, add the apple wood or peach wood just before placing the meat on the smoker. Place the pork loin in the center of the cooker. Cook the loin until you obtain an internal temperature of 145°F (63°C). It should take 2–3 hours. Start checking the internal temperature at the 1½-hour mark.

When the meat is done, remove it from the cooker and let it rest for about 30 minutes, loosely tented with aluminum foil. Slice it thinly (¼-inch [6-mm]) and serve. Trust me, this pork will be juicy, tender and delicious!

APPLE-SMOKED BABY BACK RIBS

When you think all-American barbecue, what do you think of? My first thought is baby back ribs. This is what got me started in the fun and crazy world of competition barbecue. I love ribs! I used to order them every chance I got when we would go out for dinner. Then one day I thought, *Hmm . . . I bet I could make these at home.* So, I went out and got a smoker. It was a small, red Brinkman and the temperature gauge read low, which is ideal and hot—I'm sure some of you know exactly what I'm talking about. The first set of ribs I cooked came out awful. I think there were only two boats from each rack that were even edible. It was a complete disaster! That was more than fifteen years ago. I have honed my barbecue skills since then, and have come up with a rib recipe that I can certainly be proud of. I think you'll like it, too!

SERVES: 8 • COOK TIME: 3½–4 HOURS

¼ cup (44 g) yellow mustard

2 racks loin back (baby back) ribs, membrane removed

1 cup (128 g) Barbecue Seasoning Rub (page 182)

Apple wood chips or chunks (if using chips, soak in water for about an hour)

1 cup (340 g) honey

½ cup (120 g) firmly packed brown sugar (light or dark)

4 tbsp (56 g) butter

1 cup (240 ml) Honey Barbecue Sauce (page 173)

Brush some of the yellow mustard on both sides of the ribs, just enough to lightly coat them (the purpose of the mustard is to give the rub something to stick to).

Sprinkle the meat with the rub. A good overall dusting on both sides of the ribs is all you will need. Let the ribs sit for about 1 hour before cooking to allow the meat to come to room temperature.

While the ribs are resting, preheat your smoker for low and slow cooking, about 250°F (121°C). For this recipe, I like to use my insulated cabinet smoker. If you are using an uninsulated bullet-style cooker (like a WSM), pay attention to the water pan and your fuel to make sure it doesn't run out of water or fuel and cook on the top cooking grate.

Put the wood chips or chunks on the smoker, then put the ribs on the grate, meat side up. Let them cook for about 2½ hours.

After the ribs cook for 2½ hours, take a couple sheets of heavy-duty aluminum foil and place ½ cup (170 g) of the honey, ¼ cup (60 g) of the brown sugar and 2 tablespoons (28 g) of the butter on each sheet. Place the ribs on top, meat side down. On the back side of the ribs pour some of the barbecue sauce, and wrap tightly. Place the ribs back on the smoker for another hour, or until done. You will know they are done when you can see the meat shrink from the bone about ¼–½-inch (6-13-mm).

Remove from the smoker, open the foil and let the ribs vent for 10 minutes. Take the ribs out of the foil and glaze them with the leftover juices and let them rest for 15–20 minutes, then cut them up and serve.

(continued)

Placing ribs meat side down in foil wrap.

Drizzling brown sugar and honey.

Adding butter.

Adding BBQ sauce.

Wrapping ribs to finish cooking.

APPLE-SMOKED BABY BACK RIBS (CONTINUED)

PROPERLY COOKED RIBS

I know this may come as a shock to most of you, but properly cooked ribs should not fall off the bone. If they do, what you have is really expensive pulled pork. A properly cooked rib will bite cleanly from the bone with your teeth, and still have some texture—similar to that of a perfectly cooked steak. Here are a few different ways to tell whether the ribs are done:

1. The meat has shrunk up on the bone by about ¼–½-inch (6–13-mm).

2. The bend test: using a pair of tongs, grab the middle of the rack and lift up. The ribs should bend about 90 degrees and almost break apart.

3. The twist test: put your thumb on one bone and your four fingers on another and move your hand in opposite directions. The meat should start to separate when done.

4. Use a toothpick and pierce in between two bones; if it goes in with little or no effort, the ribs are done.

COUNTRY-STYLE RIBS WITH JERK SEASONING

Country-style ribs are the meatiest of all the ribs. They are cut from the sirloin, or rib end, of the pork loin. These pork ribs are perfect for those who want to use a knife and fork, but you can certainly eat them with your hands if you don't mind getting a little bit messy. It wouldn't be good barbecue without a little bit of sauce on your shirt, right? For this recipe, I mix Dr Pepper with jerk seasoning. The sweetness of the soda works well with the spices in the jerk seasoning.

SERVES: 6–8 • COOK TIME: 3–4 HOURS

8½ cups (2 L) Dr Pepper

½ cup (144 g) kosher salt

3 lb (1.4 kg) country-style ribs

1 cup (128 g) Jamaican Jerk Seasoning (page 183)

3–4 chunks cherry wood

In a large pitcher, mix the Dr Pepper and salt together until the salt is completely dissolved. Place the ribs in a gallon (3.8 L) zip-top bag and add the Dr Pepper brine. Let the ribs sit in the brine for a minimum of 2 hours, or up to a maximum of 8 hours.

Remove the ribs from the brine. Discard the used brine. Rinse off the ribs and pat them dry with a paper towel.

Lay out the ribs on a sheet pan (or cookie sheet) and liberally coat the ribs with the jerk seasoning.

For this recipe, I like to use my non-insulated bullet-style smoker. Fire up your smoker to 250°F (121°C). Add your cherry wood just before putting the meat on. The thing I like about cherry wood on pork is that it not only gives the meat you're cooking a nice flavor, but it also helps create a really nice dark mahogany color. If you are using an uninsulated bullet-style cooker (like a WSM), pay attention to the water pan and your fuel to make sure it doesn't run out of water or fuel and cook on the top cooking grate.

Place the meat on the cooking grate and cook for 2–3 hours, or until an internal temperature of 180°F (82°C) is reached.

Next, transfer the ribs to a half-size disposable aluminum pan, cover with foil and put back on the cooker for another hour.

Remove the meat from the cooker and remove one corner of the cover from the pan. Let the meat rest for about 30 minutes. Serve, enjoy and try not to get any sauce on your shirt.

CHINESE FIVE-SPICE MARINATED RIBS

I love Chinese ribs and order them any chance I get when I go out for Chinese food. These ribs are different than the traditional Southern-style ribs in that they don't have a dry rub applied to them, and they are marinated, which is the key to their flavor. They are finished off with a simple, sweet glaze that gives you that familiar Chinese-rib taste.

FOR THE MARINADE

⅓ cup (110 g) honey

¼ cup (60 ml) Chinese rice wine or dry sherry

¼ cup (60 g) ketchup

2 tbsp (30 ml) Sriracha

2 tbsp (40 g) hoisin sauce

2 tbsp (30 ml) soy sauce

2 tsp (10 ml) sesame oil

¼ cup (24 g) minced garlic

1 tbsp (6 g) grated ginger

1 tsp (3 g) Chinese five-spice powder

FOR THE SAUCE

⅓ cup (80 ml) Chinese-style barbecue sauce, such as Ah-So sauce

2 tbsp (30 ml) hot water

FOR THE RIBS

2 racks spareribs, membranes removed

2 tbsp (16 g) sesame seeds for garnish

To make the marinade, mix all the ingredients in a bowl and set aside.

To make the sauce, mix the ingredients in a bowl and set aside.

Place the ribs in large (2½-gallon [9.5-L]) zip-top bag and pour the marinade over them. Shake to coat the ribs. Place the bag in the fridge and let marinate for at least 4 hours (flipping over after 2 hours for even coating). Marinating overnight would be best to get that real Chinese-restaurant flavor into the ribs.

For this recipe, I like to use an insulated cabinet smoker. Fire up your smoker to 250°F–275°F (121°C–135°C). We won't be using any additional smoke wood for this recipe, just the smoke coming from the charcoal. We want a very subtle smoke flavor for this dish, and the ribs would be overpowered by using additional smoke wood. If you are using an uninsulated bullet-style cooker (like a WSM), pay attention to the water pan and your fuel to make sure it doesn't run out of water or fuel and cook on the top cooking grate.

After the ribs have finished marinating, remove them from the plastic bag and discard the used marinade. Place the ribs on the cooking grate, meat side up and cook for about 3½ hours.

After about 3½ hours, brush the sauce over the ribs. Cook for 15 minutes, then brush the sauce over the ribs again and cook for another 15 minutes.

Remove the ribs from the cooker. Cut the ribs, sprinkle with some sesame seeds and serve.

Glazing ribs.

Sprinkling with sesame seeds.

AWARD-WINNING GRILLED PORK CHOPS

This recipe is one of my personal favorites, so I just had to include it again in this book. This is the recipe that garnered my very first first-place trophy in competition barbecue! It is such a simple pork chop recipe, yet when cooked properly it's one of the tastiest pork chops you will ever eat. The caramelization of the sugars in the apple butter glaze is what really hits your taste buds!

SERVES: 4 • COOK TIME: APPROXIMATELY 30 MINUTES

1 cup (240 g) apple butter

½ cup (120 ml) apple cider

2 tbsp (30 ml) apple cider vinegar

½ cup (64 g) Smokin' Hoggz All-Purpose Rub (page 181)

4 double-boned pork chops, frenched (see Note)

1 (12-oz [355-ml]) bottle steak marinade, such as Lawry's Steak & Chop Marinade

In a medium bowl, combine the apple butter, apple cider, apple cider vinegar and 1 tablespoon (8 g) of the all-purpose rub and mix well; set aside until ready to use.

Place the pork chops in a gallon (3.8-L) zip-top bag and add the bottle of steak marinade. Let the chops marinate in the fridge for at least 4 hours; overnight would be best.

Remove the chops from the marinade. Discard the marinade and pat the chops dry using paper towels. Apply a generous coating of the rub, and really work it into the meat.

I'll be using my charcoal grill for this and setting it up for two-zone cooking. Fill up a charcoal chimney with hardwood lump charcoal and light it. When flames start coming out of the top of the chimney, the coals are ready. Dump onto one side of the cooker. Keep the other side clear for indirect cooking.

Once the charcoal is ready, place the chops on the cooking grate on the direct-heat zone. Cook for about 3 minutes. Flip and cook for an additional 3 minutes. Move the chops to the indirect-heat zone. Place the lid back on the grill, and continue to cook for an additional 20 minutes, or until you reach an internal temperature of 145°F (63°C).

Remove the chops from the grill and let rest for about 10 minutes. They are now ready to serve.

NOTE: Frenching is a technique where the rib bone is exposed and all the meat is removed from the bone. You can do it, but if you don't feel comfortable doing it, you can have your butcher do it for you free of charge. Having the pork chops frenched not only looks impressive on the plate but also, if you so desire, you can pick it up with your hands and eat the chop like it's a giant rib!

HONEY-GLAZED SMOKED PORK CHOPS

Smoked pork chops are just as delicious and mouthwatering as the high-heat grilled version—perhaps even more so! The difference, apart from the smokier flavor, is these guys will take about 2 hours to cook. Trust me, though: it is *so worth the wait.*

SERVES: 4 • COOK TIME: APPROXIMATELY 2 HOURS

1 tbsp (8 g) black pepper

1 tsp (3 g) garlic powder

1 tsp (3 g) chili powder

4 pork chops (1½" [1.3-cm] thick)

Kosher salt

3-4 chunks apple wood

½ cup (170 g) honey

Mix the pepper, garlic and chili powder together in a small bowl and set aside until ready to use.

Generously coat both sides of the pork chops with kosher salt. Place the chops in a zip-top bag and put them in the fridge overnight. Take them out of the fridge and rinse. Pat dry with a paper towel. Dust the pork chops with the black pepper seasoning. You don't want to use too much because you want the smoke to adhere to the surface and penetrate into the meat.

For this recipe, I like to use my insulated cabinet smoker. Bring the smoker up to 250°F (121°C). Add the apple wood just before putting the meat on the smoker. If you are using an uninsulated bullet-style cooker (like a WSM), pay attention to the water pan and your fuel to make sure it doesn't run out of water or fuel and cook on the top cooking grate.

Once the cooker is up to temperature, place the pork chops on the middle rack. If you are using a non-insulated bullet-style smoker, place the meat on the top grate.

Cook until you get an internal temperature of about 130°F (54°C), then drizzle and brush some of the honey over the pork chops. Do this every 15 minutes until the chops reach an internal temperature of 145°F (63°C).

Remove the chops from the smoker and let rest for about 5 minutes. The chops are ready to eat, and you're about to learn that they were worth the wait. Enjoy!

BACON-WRAPPED PORK TENDERLOIN

Pork tenderloin is the filet mignon of pork. It's a very lean piece of meat and can dry out very quickly when overcooked. So, you should cook tenderloin over high heat and you should cook it quickly. This is a simple recipe that delivers some great flavor because anything wrapped in bacon is just plain old good!

SERVES: 3 • COOK TIME: 30 MINUTES

1 Bacon Weave (page 42)

¼ cup (32 g) Smokin' Hoggz All-Purpose Rub (page 181)

1 apple, thinly sliced (about ⅛" [3-mm] thick)

1 (1½-lb [680-g]) pork tenderloin

1 cup (240 ml) Honey Barbecue Sauce (page 173)

I will be using my charcoal grill for this cook and setting it up for two-zone cooking. Fill up a charcoal chimney with hardwood lump charcoal and light it. When flames start coming out of the top of the chimney, the coals are ready. Dump onto one side of the cooker. Keep the other side clear for indirect cooking.

Lay out a sheet of heavy-duty foil and spray one side with nonstick cooking spray. Place the Bacon Weave on the foil and season with some of the rub. Lay some apple slices in the center of the Bacon Weave. Place the tenderloin on top of the apple slices. Put some more apple slices on top of the tenderloin and dust with some rub. Roll the bacon weave around the tenderloin and make sure the seam is on the bottom. Season the outside with more rub. Because we will be flipping the tenderloin to cook it over high heat, it's a good idea to use a couple of toothpicks to secure the Bacon Weave to the meat. Otherwise, you take a chance that the Bacon Weave could unwrap.

Remove the bacon-wrapped tenderloin from the foil. Place the tenderloin directly over the coals and place the cover on the grill. Cook the tenderloin for about 3 minutes. Flip the tenderloin, but do not place it back on the same spot—place it on another hot spot. Cook for another 3 minutes. The reason why you don't want to put it back in the same spot is that the place where the meat was has cooled down and you want all the heat you can get, so use a fresh spot.

Now move the tenderloin to the indirect-heat zone. Baste once with the barbecue sauce, place the lid on the grill, and continue cooking until you get an internal temperature of 150°F (66°C), about 20 minutes.

Remove the tenderloin from the heat and let rest for about 10 minutes, then cut into ½-inch (1.3-cm) slices and serve.

CRANBERRY AND GOAT CHEESE-STUFFED TENDERLOIN

I stuffed this tenderloin with dried cranberries, apricots and goat cheese, and *wow!* The sweetness of the dried fruit paired with tangy goat cheese was out of this world. It was so simple and wickedly delicious!

SERVES: APPROXIMATELY 6–8 • COOK TIME: APPROXIMATELY 30 MINUTES

2 (1-lb [455-g]) pork tenderloins

Salt and pepper

2 tbsp (30 ml) olive oil, plus more for coating the tenderloin

1 medium shallot, chopped

½ cup (75 g) dried cranberries

½ cup (65 g) chopped dried apricots

1 cup (150 g) goat cheese, softened

I like to use my charcoal grill for this cook and set it up for two-zone cooking. Fill up a charcoal chimney with hardwood lump charcoal and light it. When flames start coming out of the top of the chimney, the coals are ready. Dump onto one side of the cooker. Keep the other side clear for indirect cooking.

Using a sharp knife, make an incision halfway through the length of the tenderloins, so they open like a book. Be careful not to cut all the way through. Season the inside of each tenderloin with salt and pepper, then set aside.

In a skillet, heat the olive oil over medium heat. Sauté the shallot, cranberries and apricots until softened, about 5 minutes.

Spread half of the goat cheese in the center of one side of each tenderloin. Spoon half the cranberry mixture on top of the cheese on each tenderloin. Close up the other side of the tenderloin using butcher's string. Tie the string around the pork every 1-inch (2.5-cm). Coat the outside of the tenderloin with olive oil and season with salt and pepper.

Place the tenderloin directly over the coals and put the cover on. Cook for 3–5 minutes. Flip the tenderloin, but do not place it back on the same spot—place it on another hot spot. Cook for another 3–5 minutes. The reason why you don't want to put it back in the same spot is the place where the meat was has cooled down and you want all the heat you can get, so use a fresh spot.

Now move the tenderloin to the indirect-heat zone. Place the lid on the grill, and continue cooking until you obtain an internal temperature of 150°F (66°C), about 20 minutes.

Remove the tenderloin from the heat and let rest for about 10 minutes, then cut into ½–1 inch (1.3–2.5 cm) slices and serve.

CORNBREAD-STUFFED PORK LOIN

Pork loin is a tender piece of meat located just underneath the baby back ribs. Some would even call the loin "the prime rib of pork." This is a great piece of meat to stuff and smoke. It's very lean and cooks pretty quick. Here's one of my favorite ways to cook this wonderful piece of hog heaven—stuffed with cornbread stuffing and glazed with a little raspberry-chipotle sauce!

SERVES: 8 • COOK TIME: 2–2½ HOURS

3 chunks apple wood

1 (4-lb [1.8-kg]) pork loin

2 cups (280 g) Chourico and Cornbread Stuffing (page 88)

2-3 tbsp (30–45 ml) olive oil

½ cup (64 g) Smokin' Hoggz All-Purpose Rub (page 181)

1 (4-oz [112-g]) can chipotle peppers in adobo sauce

1 (10-oz [280-g]) jar seedless raspberry jam

For this recipe, I like to use my non-insulated bullet-style smoker, and fire it up for low and slow cooking, about 250°F (121°C). Fill the water pan about halfway with hot water and add your apple wood about 5 minutes before putting the meat on. If your cooker doesn't have a water pan, simply fill up a disposable aluminum pan and place it in the bottom of the smoker.

Trim the white "silver skin" from the pork loin. Butterfly the pork loin. The easiest way to do this is to slice it across the middle like a hot dog bun, stopping about ½-inch (1.3-cm) from cutting all the way through. Next, pile on the stuffing and close up the loin. Tie butcher's string every 1½-inches (3.8-cm) to keep the pork loin closed. Lightly coat the entire loin with olive oil. Liberally sprinkle the rub on all sides of the loin.

Place the pork loin in the smoker and smoke until the internal temperature reaches 140°F (66°C), 1½–2½ hours, depending on the thickness of the meat. I would start checking it after 1½ hours.

Finely dice 3–4 of the chipotles. Place the jam in a medium bowl and stir in the diced chipotle with about 3 tablespoons (45 ml) of the adobo sauce. Mix well, adding more chipotle sauce until the heat and taste reach your personal preference.

During the last 30 minutes of cooking, brush on the chipotle-raspberry sauce and continue cooking to help the sauce set. Remove the pork loin from the cooker and let rest for about 15 minutes. Slice the pork and serve with more sauce.

CHAPTER 5

BUTTS, SHOULDERS AND HAMS

According to some sources, hogs were fist domesticated in China about seven thousand years ago. That sure has provided a lot of time to learn the best ways to cook the different parts of the animal. For many people, the animals' butts, loins and shoulders provide the most coveted pieces of meat. While we're discussing pig parts, let me take a moment to clear up a little misconception for those of you who might still be learning about the animal's anatomy. Pork butt isn't what a lot of people seem to think it is. The butt has absolutely nothing to do with the end of the animal that takes care of business, if you know what I mean. Good to know, right?

Pork butt, also known as Boston butt, comes from the upper shoulder region of the animal's front legs, and usually contains the blade bone. Pork butt tends to have veins of fat intermingled with the lean muscle, which is referred to as marbling. When you slow cook a pork butt, these marbled layers of fat melt into the protein, adding to the texture and flavor of the meat.

Pork butt should not be confused with a picnic shoulder. Typically, a picnic shoulder is taken from the lower region of the animal's front shoulder and is thinner than a pork butt. Sometimes, you can find the picnic shoulder still connected to the pork butt, which is known as a whole shoulder. Pretty straightforward stuff once you understand it, right?

Lastly, I'd like to talk about the hind shoulder, and the one dish we all know that uses the hind shoulder—ham. Basically, ham is just the hind shoulder that has been cured. The nitrates in the curing salt are what create the pink color most people associated with ham. At one time, many families could only afford to purchase the more expensive choice cuts of meat on rare occasions. Today, the tradition of having ham as the main entrée at holiday gatherings is most likely related to the fact that the hind shoulder is one of the more expensive cuts of pork. Similarly, the fact that the choice cuts of meat all come from the upper regions of the animal is why some people claim that the expression "high off the hog" refers to living the good life.

This chapter contains some of my favorite recipes for butts, shoulders and hams. I hope that when you make any of these recipes, you'll surround yourself with family and close friends—that way, you'll truly be living the good life. Enjoy!

COMPETITION PORK

In competition barbecue, the meat used in the pork category comes from the pork shoulder. Pork shoulder is usually made up of two cuts: the shoulder and the butt. Pork shoulder or butt has a very high intramuscular fat content. This fat provides a challenge during the cooking process, along with the potential reward of delicious barbecued pork. The cooking challenge is learning to render the fat without overcooking the meat. When the challange is overcome, the result is a tender, moist and flavorful product that is hard to beat. I know I included a competition pork recipe in my other cookbook, but I want to share some of the small changes I've made to the way I make my competition pork. You will need a basic 2-ounce (60-ml) injector for this recipe, which you can purchase at most supermarkets or department stores.

SERVES: ABOUT 20 • COOK TIME 10–12 HOURS

2 (8–10-lb [3.6–4.5-kg]) Boston butts, bone-in

1 recipe Pork Injection (page 129)

½ cup (88 g) yellow or honey mustard

2 cups (256 g) Whole-Hog Dry Rub (page 166)

2 chunks apple wood

2 chunks sugar maple wood

1 recipe Pork Braise (page 128)

1½ cups (355 ml) Smokin' Hoggz Barbecue Sauce or Honey BBQ Sauce (page 173)

1½ cups (355 ml) barbecue sauce, such as original flavor Head Country Bar-B-Q Sauce

Trim the butts of any extra or loose fat. Keep the fat cap on; this protects the butt during the cooking process and helps retain moisture. Remember, fat is flavor.

Inject half of the injection liquid into each butt by inserting the needle and pushing the plunger. Make sure the majority of the injection goes into the muscle opposite the bone (a.k.a. money muscle) and the muscles around the bone.

Rub down the entire butt with the mustard. You don't need to use a lot of mustard. All the mustard is doing is creating a surface to which the rub will adhere.

After you coat the butt with mustard, generously apply the rub. Wrap the butts in plastic wrap and place them in the fridge until an hour before they go on the smoker.

Remove the pork butts from the refrigerator and apply another generous coating of rub. Let the meat sit at room temperature until ready to go on the smoker.

For this recipe, I like to use my insulated cabinet smoker. Fire up your smoker and get it ready for low and slow cooking, about 250°F (121°C). If you are using an uninsulated bullet-style cooker (like a WSM), pay attention to the water pan and your fuel to make sure it doesn't run out of water or fuel and cook on the top cooking grate.

After the temperature stabilizes, add the apple wood and sugar maple wood about 15 minutes before you start cooking the meat. Place the butts on the smoker grate, fat side up. Depending on the smoker you are using, you might be able to get both butts on one cooking grate. If you have a bullet-style cooker, you can arrange the butts with one on the top grate and one on the bottom grate. If you are using an insulated cabinet cooker, and have a narrow cooker, place the butts on the grates front to back so that the money muscles face each other. If your cooker is wider, place them side-to-side with the money muscles facing the door. You don't want to overcook this part of the butt (the money muscles). Arranging the butts as I've described will help prevent the money muscle from drying out. Cook the butts to an internal temperature of 160°F–170°F (71°C–77°C), about 6 hours.

(continued)

Lay out 2 sheets of heavy-duty aluminum foil (big enough to fully wrap each butt). Place each butt on a sheet of foil fat side down and pour half of the braise onto each butt. Wrap the butts completely with foil and return them to the smoker. Cook until the internal temperature in the money muscle reaches 185°F–187°F (85°C–86°C), about 2–3 hours.

Remove the butts, cut the money muscles off both butts, and place them into a half-size pan. Take the juice from one of the foil pouches and pour over the muscles. Mix the two barbecue sauces together, and brush the top of the money muscles with the sauce. Cover with foil and place the half-size pan into a warming box (such as a Cambro) or dry, empty cooler (without ice) until ready for presentation. Wrap the remaining butts back up and place on the smoker. Continue cooking to an internal temperature of 195°F (91°C), about 2–3 hours.

Remove the butts from the smoker, open the foil and allow the steam to dissipate, about 10 minutes. This helps stop the cooking process. Apply a coating of the barbecue sauce mixture to the top surface of the butts. Close the foil and let rest for a minimum of 1 hour in a warming box or dry, empty cooler lined with cloth towels.

When ready to serve, heat some of the barbecue sauce mixture in a small pan. Pull some chunks from around the bone and dip them in the heated barbecue sauce. Remove the money muscles and slice into ½-inch (1.3-cm) medallions. Present, serve and enjoy!

PORK BRAISE

The world of competition barbecue is all about layering flavors. The judges who score entries usually take only one or two bites of the meat you present to them. This means you don't have much of an opportunity to really wow them. One way to help your entry stand out from those of the other competitors is to successfully layer flavors. Using this braise when you wrap a pork butt in foil for the final part of the cooking process will add an interesting layer of flavor to the finished dish.

MAKES: APPROXIMATELY 2 CUPS (475 ML)

1 (12-oz [355-ml]) bottle of pork marinade, such as Stubb's Pork Marinade, strained

½ cup (120 ml) apple juice or white grape juice

½ cup (120 ml) Smokin' Hoggz Barbecue Sauce or Honey BBQ Sauce (page 173)

1 tbsp (8 g) Whole-Hog Dry Rub (page 166)

Mix all the ingredients in a bowl and heat just before using.

PORK INJECTION

Injection is a culinary process that infuses flavor and moisture into meat. Unlike the marinating process, in which liquid typically penetrates the surface of the meat by about a ¼-inch (6-mm), injecting uses a syringe to insert flavor deep into the meat. The additional liquid also helps the meat retain more moisture throughout the cooking process, resulting in tender, juicy meat. Here is an injection I use for my pork butts. Phosphates improve texture and help keep the meat moist and juicy. You can usually purchase phosphates at any specialty barbecue store.

MAKES: 4 CUPS (940 ML), ENOUGH FOR 2 (8–10 LB [3.6–4.5 KG]) PORK BUTTS

1 cup (240 ml) apple juice or white grape juice

2 tbsp (36 g) kosher salt

¼ cup (60 ml) Worcestershire sauce

½ cup (120 ml) water

½ cup (120 g) brown sugar (light or dark)

1 tsp (3 g) cayenne pepper

2 tbsp (30 ml) soy sauce

¼ cup (60 ml) apple cider vinegar

¼ cup (32 g) AmesPhos phosphates

Combine all the ingredients in a bowl and stir until the salt and sugar are completely dissolved. This injection can be used with any cut of pork. Inject the meat using a basic 2-ounce (60-ml) injector, which you can purchase at most supermarkets or department stores.

PORK BURNT ENDS

Typically when you think of burnt ends, you think of the traditional Kansas City cubed and a little bit charred pieces of beef brisket brushed with sauce. Here, I will show you how to make them from boneless pork ribs—they are just as good and just as flavorful as their beef counterpart. In fact, I think these are even better, well for one reason … it's pork!!!

YIELD 4-6 SERVINGS • COOK TIME 4-5 HOURS

¼ cup (44 ml) yellow mustard

3-4 lb (1.4-1.8 kg) country style ribs (make sure they are cut from the pork butt)

1 cup (128 g) dry rub, such as Whole-Hog Dry Rub (page 166)

3 chunks cherry wood

SPICY BUTTER

1 stick butter, melted

2 tbsp (7 g) hot sauce, such as Franks Red Hot Sauce

Apply a coat of yellow mustard to all sides of the meat and sprinkle a generous amount of Whole-Hog Dry Rub onto all sides. Allow the meat to rest for about 20-30 minutes until it starts to get a "wet" look.

For this recipe, I like to use my uninsulated bullet-style cooker. Fire up your smoker to about 250°F (121°C). If you are using an uninsulated bullet style cooker, make sure to fill your water pan with about 1 gallon (3.78 L) of hot water and pay attention that it doesn't run out of water. Add the cherry wood chunks just before putting the ribs directly on the top grate.

You will want to smoke the ribs for 3 hours at 250°F (121°C) or until the meat reaches an internal temperature of 170°F (77°C) in the center. Take the meat off the cooker and let it cool for about 30 minutes before cutting into 1-inch by 1-inch (2.5 x 2.5-cm) cubes.

Use an injector to inject each piece with butter until the butter runs out of the meat; place injected pieces into a disposable aluminum half-pan. Sprinkle on more rub to create a nice bark all over.

Return the pan of injected pieces of pork back into the smoker, again on the top grate.

Continue to cook for about 2 hours or until they get nice and crusty or to your liking.

Stir occasionally while they cook.

Serve immediately on toothpicks as an appetizer.

PORK-LOADED BARBECUED BEANS

You can't have barbecue without having some sort of great side dish, like my Pork-Loaded Barbecue Beans! What a great way to use some leftover shredded pork and bacon. (I know, I know, there's never any leftover bacon, so you must intentionally save some to make this dish.) Being from Boston, I certainly better know how to make baked beans. Try these for your next gathering—you'll be glad you did!

SERVES: 8 • COOK TIME: APPROXIMATELY 2–3 HOURS

2 (28-oz [784-g]) cans baked beans, such as B&M Original Baked Beans, drained

1 cup (240 ml) Smokin' Hoggz Barbecue Sauce or Honey BBQ sauce (page 173)

½ sweet onion, diced

1 cup (80 g) diced and cooked Maple-Smoked Pork Belly (page 18) or any bacon

1 lb (455 g) Simple Pulled Pork (page 133)

2 tbsp (16 g) Smokin' Hoggz All-Purpose Rub (page 181)

1–2 jalapeño peppers, finely chopped (optional)

2 chunks apple wood

For this recipe, I like to use my insulated cabinet smoker, cooking at 250°F–275°F (121°C–135°C). I'm also going to add about a gallon (3.8 L) of hot water to the water pan. If your cooker doesn't have a water pan, simply fill up a disposable aluminum pan and place it in the bottom of the smoker. If you are using an uninsulated bullet-style cooker (like a WSM), pay attention to the water pan and your fuel to make sure it doesn't run out of water or fuel and cook on the top cooking grate.

Combine all the ingredients in a half-size disposable aluminum pan and place on the top rack of the smoker. Add the apple wood chunks and cook for about 2 hours, uncovered; stir after about 1 hour to incorporate some of that great smoke flavor from the apple wood and continue cooking. Stir the beans again after another hour, then cover with heavy-duty foil and cook for an additional hour.

Remove from the cooker and let rest for about 30 minutes. Serve as a great side dish with your favorite barbecued meats.

SIMPLE PULLED PORK

Sometimes, you just want a plain old, tasty serving of shredded pork, whether it's on a sandwich roll or added to some other dish, and you don't always want the extra flavors from dry rubs and sauce. Sometimes, you just want to taste that nice pork flavor—plain and simple. Trust me, after a while, you'll want to give this recipe a try and you'll be surprised what a little bit of salt and pepper will do to bring out the flavor of the pork.

SERVES: 15 • COOK TIME: APPROXIMATELY 8–10 HOURS

1 (8-lb [3.6-kg]) pork butt

Olive oil

Salt and pepper

4–6 chunks apple wood

½ cup (120 ml) apple juice

Trim off any loose fat on the pork butt, drizzle on some olive oil and coat the entire butt. Season with salt and pepper.

For this recipe, I like to use my insulated cabinet smoker. Wait for the smoker to come up to 250°F (121°C), and add the apple wood just before you put the meat on. If you are using an uninsulated bullet-style cooker (like a WSM), pay attention to the water pan and your fuel to make sure it doesn't run out of water or fuel and cook on the top cooking grate.

A cabinet smoker cooks food using a reverse flow effect. Heat and smoke travel up the interior sides of the smoker, and then back downward from the top of the smoker. The air flows over the meat, cooking and flavoring the food, then exits the bottom of the smoker. I like to cook my meat with the fat cap facing up to protect the meat from the direct flow of heat and smoke. Also, as the meat is cooking, the fat cap will render down over the meat, which also helps with keeping the meat moist and juicy—self-basting, you could say.

Cook the pork until you get an internal temperature of 160°F–170°F (71°C–77°C), about 7 hours. At this point, lay out a large sheet of heavy-duty aluminum foil. Place the butt on the foil with the fat cap down, pour the apple juice over the butt and then wrap it up tightly. Place back onto the cooker and cook until you get an internal temperature of about 195°F (91°C), which should take 2–3 hours.

Remove from the cooker and open the foil to allow the steam to escape for 5–10 minutes. This will help stop the cooking process. Wrap it back up and place into a dry empty cooler or warming box (such as a Cambro) and let rest for 1–1½ hours.

After the meat is done resting, you can begin to pull it apart and shred it, throwing out all the gristle and fat. Save the liquid from the foil and strain it. Add the strained liquid back to the meat in a bowl. You are now ready to use the shredded pork for whatever you want!

PICNIC PORK SHOULDER WITH CRISPY SKIN

There are two cuts of meat that make up a whole shoulder: the pork butt and the picnic shoulder. The picnic shoulder is located on the bottom region of the shoulder, closer to the hoof and usually has the hide still attached. Instead of getting those soft and stringy shredded pieces of meat, you'll have meaty chunks of pork that you can literally pull apart with your fingers. What I like to do after I finish cooking this is hit it with some high heat on my charcoal grill to get the outer skin (hide) nice and crispy. Crispy pork skin! Yeah, it's good!

SERVES: 15–20 • COOK TIME: APPROXIMATELY 10–12 HOURS

FOR THE BASIC INJECTION

½ cup (120 ml) apple juice

¼ cup (60 ml) water

¼ cup (50 g) sugar

2 tbsp (36 g) kosher salt

2 tbsp (30 ml) Worcestershire sauce

1 tbsp (15 ml) apple cider vinegar

1 meat injector

FOR THE PICNIC SHOULDER

1 (8-lb [3.6-kg]) picnic shoulder

Olive oil

½ cup (64 g) Barbecue Seasoning Rub (page 182)

4-6 chunks apple wood

To make the injection, mix all the ingredients in a bowl until the sugar and salt have dissolved, then cover and store in the fridge until ready to use.

Trim off any loose fat on the picnic shoulder. Using a meat injector, inject the picnic shoulder in several places. Use all of the injection mixture. This adds flavor to the picnic shoulder and helps the meat retain moisture. Coat the entire picnic shoulder with olive oil. Season the picnic shoulder liberally with the barbecue seasoning.

For this recipe, I like to use my insulated cabinet smoker, and add about 1 gallon (3.8 L) of hot water to the water pan. If your cooker doesn't have a water pan, simply fill up a disposable aluminum pan and place it in the bottom of the smoker. If you are using an uninsulated bullet-style cooker (like a WSM), pay attention to the water pan and your fuel to make sure it doesn't run out of water or fuel and cook on the top cooking grate! When the smoker stabilizes at 250°F (121°C), add the apple wood, and place the picnic shoulder on the middle rack with the larger surface of skin facing up.

A cabinet-style smoker cooks food using a reverse flow effect. Heat and smoke travel up the interior sides of the smoker, and then back downward from the top of the smoker. The air flows over the meat, cooking and flavoring the food, then exits the bottom of the smoker. I like to cook picnic shoulder with the majority of the outer skin (hide) facing up to protect the meat from the direct flow of heat and smoke. As the meat cooks, the fat under the skin renders down into the picnic shoulder, which helps keep the meat moist and juicy—self-basting, you could say. Cook the pork to an internal temperature of 190°F (88°C), about 10 hours. Remove from the smoker and loosely tent with heavy-duty foil.

While the picnic shoulder is resting, fire up your charcoal grill for direct grilling (this should take about 15 minutes). Simply light the charcoal using a charcoal chimney, and dump the hot coals into the grill. Create a uniform layer of charcoal and cook your food directly above the heat source. Flip the picnic shoulder a quarter turn every 2-3 minutes, until the skin becomes nice and crispy. Try to avoid burning it.

Once the skin is crispy, remove from the grill and loosely tent with foil for about 30 minutes. Using a pair of heat-resistant gloves, shred the picnic shoulder into a bowl. Pour any drippings into the bowl. Don't forget to save some of that nice crispy skin to snack on!

PULLED PORK TACOS, TWO WAYS

Shredded or pulled pork is one of my favorite barbecue foods. There are so many wonderful and different ways you can use it—in a pulled pork sandwich, in barbecued baked beans or even on a pizza. In this recipe, I am going to show you how to use some leftover pork to create flavorful tacos.

METHOD 1—SERVES: 6–8 • PREP TIME: 15 MINUTES
METHOD 2—SERVES: 6–8 • PREP TIME: 15 MINUTES

FOR METHOD 1

12–16 (4" [10-cm]) flour tortillas

4 lb (1.8 kg) Simple Pulled Pork (page 133)

4 cups (400 g) coleslaw

Barbecue sauce, for drizzling

FOR METHOD 2

1 cup (240 g) sour cream

¼ cup (4 g) chopped fresh cilantro

Zest and juice of 1 lime

Salt and pepper

12–16 (4" [10-cm]) flour tortillas

4 lb (3.6 kg) Simple Pulled Pork (page 133)

4 cups (280 g) shredded lettuce

2 cups (480 g) pico de gallo or chunky salsa

FOR METHOD 1

To assemble these tacos, take one of the tortillas and lay it out flat. Place about ¼ pound (112 g) of pork in the center of the tortilla. Top with ¼ cup (85 g) of slaw and drizzle with barbecue sauce. Repeat for the remaining tortillas and serve.

FOR METHOD 2

In a bowl, combine the sour cream, cilantro and lime zest and juice and mix well. Add salt and pepper to taste. Keep in the fridge until ready to use.

To assemble these tacos, take one of the tortillas and lay it out flat. Place about ¼ pound (112 g) of pork in the center of the tortilla. Add ¼ cup (18 g) of shredded lettuce and 2 tablespoons (30 g) of pico de gallo, then top with a dollop of the sour cream mixture. Repeat for the remaining tortillas and serve.

PULLED PORK EGG ROLLS

Here is another awesome recipe that uses leftover pulled pork. The crunch from the crispy egg roll and the sweetness from the Peach Dipping Sauce will surely make this a huge hit at your next party.

MAKES: 20 EGG ROLLS • COOK TIME: APPROXIMATELY 15 MINUTES

1 gallon (3.8 L) cooking oil (I like peanut oil)

1 egg

¼ cup (60 ml) water

5 cups (1200 g) Simple Pulled Pork (page 133)

2 cups (480 g) Honey Barbecue Sauce (page 173)

1 (16-oz [455-g]) package egg roll wrappers

5 cups (600 g) shredded pepper Jack cheese

FOR THE PEACH DIPPING SAUCE

¾ cup (180 g) peach preserves

3 tbsp (45 ml) rice wine vinegar

2 tbsp (22 g) Dijon mustard

1 tbsp (6 g) grated ginger

1 tsp (2 g) red pepper flakes

The egg rolls will be deep-fried using a charcoal grill and direct heat. Set up the grill for two-zone cooking. Fill up a charcoal chimney with hardwood lump charcoal and light it. When flames start coming out of the top of the chimney, the coals are ready. Dump onto one side of the cooker. Keep the other side clear for indirect cooking. This setup is so that if the oil gets too hot you can move the pot to the indirect-heat zone.

Once the hot coals are in place, put a Dutch oven on the grate on the direct-heat zone and add the cooking oil. You only want to fill the Dutch oven about halfway with oil, so you may not need to use the whole gallon (3.8 L) of cooking oil. Heat the oil until it reaches 350°F (177°C) on a candy thermometer.

Meanwhile, mix together the egg and water in a bowl and set aside. This will be used to seal the edges of the egg rolls.

In a large bowl, mix together the pork and 1 cup (240 ml) of the barbecue sauce, and set aside until ready to use.

Lay out an egg roll wrapper on a flat surface with one of the corners toward you. Dip a brush into the egg wash and brush just the outer edges of the egg roll wrapper. Place about ¼ cup (35 g) of cheese on the bottom half of the wrapper. Place ¼ cup (20 g) of shredded pork on top of the cheese, making sure none of the pork hits the edges of the egg roll. If the filling touches the edges it will prevent you from getting a proper seal. Take the corner facing you and place over the pork. Roll once and fold the sides in. Continue rolling until sealed. Repeat for the remaining egg rolls.

When the oil is hot, place about 4 egg rolls in the Dutch oven at a time. Cook for 2–3 minutes, or until the egg rolls are a nice golden brown. Remove with a spider or tongs and drain on paper towels. Continue until all the egg rolls are cooked. You may need to move the Dutch oven from the direct-heat zone to the indirect-heat zone and back again to maintain the oil at an even 350°F (177°C). Bring the oil back up to temperature before adding a new batch of egg rolls. This is the key to avoiding greasy fried food.

To make the Peach Dipping Sauce, mix all the ingredients together in a bowl. Serve with the egg rolls.

PULLED PORK PANINI

Have I ever said I love pulled pork? Well, *I love pulled pork!* I also love this panini sandwich, which has become a staple in my house, especially with all the leftover pork we have after a barbecue competition. The key to this sandwich is the Hoffman's cheddar cheese. It melts so nicely and really blends in with the pork. Go ahead and try it for yourself!

SERVES: 4 • COOK TIME: APPROXIMATELY 10 MINUTES PER SANDWICH

Cooking oil

8 slices panini bread

16 slices white cheddar cheese, such as Hoffman's

2 lb (910 g) Simple Pulled Pork (page 133)

1 small red onion, thinly sliced

1 cup (240 ml) Bourbon Barbecue Sauce (page 174)

Set up a charcoal grill for two-zone cooking. Fill up a charcoal chimney with hardwood lump charcoal and light it. When flames start coming out of the top of the chimney, the coals are ready. Dump onto one side of the cooker. Keep the other side clear for indirect cooking. Wrap a brick in heavy-duty aluminum foil.

Drizzle a cast-iron pan with cooking oil and place the pan on the cooking grate on the direct-heat zone. Let the pan heat up for about 5 minutes, then move over to the indirect heat zone. The reason you want to move the pan to the indirect-heat zone is so you don't burn the oil. When you move the pan to the indirect-heat zone, the pan will stay hot, but the oil is less likely to burn.

To assemble the sandwiches, lay out 2 pieces of the bread. Place 2 slices of cheese on each half of the bread. Top with ½ pound (225 g) of shredded pork. Put 3–4 slices of onion on top of the pork and drizzle with the barbecue sauce. Top with the other slice of bread. Repeat for the other 3 sandwiches.

Move the hot pan back onto the direct-heat zone. Place the sandwich in the center of the pan and put the brick wrapped in foil on top of the sandwich. You only want to cook 1 sandwich at a time. Cook for about 5 minutes. Flip and cook for an additional 5 minutes. If the pan gets too hot, just move it to the indirect-heat zone for a minute or two. Remove the sandwich from the pan and start cooking the remaining sandwiches.

Cut each sandwich in half, serve and smile.

THREE-PORK CUBAN SANDWICH

Traditionally, the Cuban sandwich is made with roasted pork loin and ham. Because I like to mess around in the kitchen, I am kicking things up a little bit. This take on the Cuban uses three meats from the smoker: home-cured pork belly, smoked pork loin and shredded pork shoulder. Yeah, this sandwich will have you floating on a cloud!

SERVES: 4 • COOK TIME: APPROXIMATELY 10 MINUTES PER SANDWICH

Cooking oil

4 Cuban rolls (if you can't find Cuban rolls, a ciabatta roll will be totally fine)

½ cup (120 g) mayonnaise

½ cup (88 g) yellow mustard

8 slices Swiss cheese

1 lb (455 g) Simple Pulled Pork (page 133)

1 lb (455 g) Simple Spiced Pork Loin (page 107), sliced

1 lb (455 g) Pepper-Crusted Pork Belly (page 17), sliced

4 whole dill pickles, thinly sliced lengthwise

Set up a charcoal grill for two-zone cooking. Fill up a charcoal chimney with hardwood lump charcoal and light it. When flames start coming out of the top of the chimney, the coals are ready. Dump onto one side of the cooker. Keep the other side clear for indirect cooking. Wrap a brick in heavy-duty aluminum foil.

Drizzle a cast-iron pan with cooking oil and place the pan on the cooking grate on the direct heat zone. Let the pan heat up for about 5 minutes, then move over to the indirect heat zone. (The reason you want to move the pan to the indirect heat zone is so you don't burn the oil. When you move the pan to the indirect heat zone, the pan will stay hot, but the oil is less likely to burn.)

To assemble the sandwiches, cut a roll in half. On one half, spread about 2 tablespoons (30 g) of the mayo. On the other half, spread about 2 tablespoons (22 g) of the mustard. Put 1 slice of the Swiss cheese on each half. Place ¼ pound (112 g) each of the pulled pork, pork loin and pork belly on one half and top with one of the sliced pickles. Place the other half of the roll on top to complete the sandwich. Repeat for the other 3 sandwiches.

Move the hot pan back onto the direct-heat zone. Place the sandwich in the center of the pan and put the brick wrapped in aluminum foil on top of the sandwich. You only want to cook 1 sandwich at a time. Cook for about 5 minutes. Flip and cook for an additional 5 minutes. If the pan gets too hot, just move it to the indirect-heat zone for a minute or two. Remove from the pan and start cooking the remaining sandwiches.

Cut each sandwich in half, eat and let the happy memories begin.

SMOKED AND STUFFED CROWN PORK ROAST

Perfect for a celebratory gathering, a crown roast of pork is formed by tying the rib section into a circle. The roast is seasoned with a flavorful marinade that includes thyme, mustard and garlic. The extra marinade becomes the basis for a delicious sauce that I think lots of taste buds will enjoy.

SERVES: 12–14 • COOK TIME: APPROXIMATELY 2½ HOURS

1 crown pork roast, 12–14 ribs (8–10 lb [3.6–4.5 kg])

1 cup (240 ml) apple cider

2 tbsp (30 ml) apple cider vinegar

2 tbsp (22 g) Dijon mustard

1 tbsp (15 g) brown sugar (light or dark)

2 cloves garlic, minced

2 tbsp (4 g) chopped fresh thyme or rosemary

1 tsp (6 g) salt

1 tsp (2 g) coarsely ground black pepper

½ cup (120 ml) olive oil

8 cups (1120 g) stuffing of choice, prepared according to package directions

3–4 chunks apple wood

Set the pork on a flat surface. Cover the end of each bone with a small piece of foil. Transfer the roast to a very large zip-top bag (2½ gallon [9.5 L]).

In a saucepan, bring the apple cider to a boil over high heat and reduce by half, 15–20 minutes. Remove from the heat and whisk in the vinegar, mustard, brown sugar, garlic, thyme or rosemary, salt and pepper. Slowly whisk in the oil.

Pour the marinade over the roast, coating all surfaces. Seal the bag. Put it in the fridge and let sit for about 4 hours. Remove from the fridge and allow the meat to come to room temperature for about 1 hour before putting it on the grill.

Remove the meat from the bag and put into a shallow pan. Don't throw the marinade away. Pour into a saucepan and reduce it down over medium heat to make a nice gravy to pour over the roast.

For this recipe, I like to use my insulated cabinet smoker. The crown roast will be smoked in the middle of the cooker for 2–2½ hours at 325°F (163°C). If you are using an uninsulated bullet-style cooker (like a WSM), pay attention to the water pan and your fuel to make sure it doesn't run out of water or fuel and cook on the top cooking grate.

Add the apple wood just before you put the roast in the smoker. Place the pan in the smoker and cook for about 1 hour. Remove from the smoker and loosely fill the crown with the stuffing, mounding it at the top. Cover the stuffing with foil. An alternative is to cook the stuffing in a separate pan alongside the roast, but I think the final presentation looks more impressive to my guests if I cook the stuffing inside the roast.

Roast the pork for another 1½ hours. Remove the foil from the stuffing and continue to roast until the internal temperature of the meat is 150°F (66°C), about another 30 minutes. When measuring the temperature, make sure the thermometer doesn't touch bone or you will get a false reading.

Remove the pan from the smoker and let the roast rest for 15–20 minutes. Remove the foil from the bones. To serve, carve between the bones and serve with the stuffing and reduced sauce.

SWEET MUSTARD-GLAZED HAM

One of the things I love about the holiday season is that someone in my family will be cooking ham. In my family, it's just not the holidays without ham! I love that savory, salty flavor mixed in with the sweetness of the glaze. The holidays can be a pretty hectic time of the year, so to make things a little easier, I like to use a ready-to-cook ham. These hams have already been cured and partially cooked. All you have to do is finish cooking the ham to 155°F–160°F (68°C–71°C). During the cooking process, you can still add your favorite seasonings and a little bit of smoke flavor. Let the holidays begin!

SERVES: 16 • COOK TIME: 3–3½ HOURS

1 (16-lb [7.3-kg]) ready-to-cook ham

½ cup (64 g) Smokin' Hoggz All-Purpose Rub (page 181)

Sweet Mustard Ham Glaze (page 148)

3–4 chunks apple wood

Remove the ham from its packaging. The ham will probably have a thin jelly-like layer on it, so rinse it off and then pat dry with a paper towel.

Score the fat with the traditional diamond/checkerboard pattern you normally see with hams. Not only does this look great after the ham is cooked, but it also helps render the fat during the cooking process. To do this, take your knife and cut lines ¼-inch (6-mm) deep about 1-inch (2.5-cm) apart, then cut again perpendicular to the cuts you just made.

Season lightly all over with rub.

Let your ham sit out at room temperature for about 1 hour.

I like to use my non-insulated bullet-style smoker for this recipe, and fire it up to 300°F–325°F (150°C–163°C). I also like to use a foil-lined water pan (for easy cleanup) containing about ½ gallon (1.8 L) of hot water so that when some of the fat drips down from the ham into the pan it won't burn and create an off-tasting smoke. If your cooker doesn't have a water pan, simply fill up a disposable aluminum pan and place it in the bottom of the smoker.

Add your apple wood at the same time you put the ham on. Place the ham on the top rack of your cooker and cook until the internal temperature reaches 155°F (68°C). This is probably going to take about 3 hours, so start checking the temperature at the 2-hour mark. You can also start applying the glaze at the 2-hour mark, too.

When the ham reaches temperature, remove it from the smoker. Loosely tent with aluminum foil and let rest for about 30 minutes. Slice and serve.

SWEET MUSTARD HAM GLAZE

What's a holiday ham without a nice glaze, right? I'm not talking about the little packet that comes with the ham—you can throw that thing away. I'm talking about making your own sweet, flavorful glaze. You and your guests are going to love this glaze! You'll notice there is no salt in this recipe. It doesn't need any because of the salt in the ham from the curing process. What I like about this glaze is how the sweetness of the honey, the savory background flavor of the mustard, and the subtle hint of heat from the chipotle pepper combine to make a perfectly flavorful glaze for your holiday ham.

MAKES: 2 CUPS (480 ML) • COOK TIME: APPROXIMATELY 15 MINUTES

1 cup (240 ml) apple cider vinegar

½ lb (225 g) dark brown sugar

½ cup (170 g) honey

¼ cup (60 ml) pineapple juice

2 tbsp (22 g) Dijon mustard

¼ tsp chipotle powder

In a medium saucepan, heat the vinegar over medium heat, and then add the brown sugar, stirring until the sugar is dissolved. Remove from the heat, add the remaining ingredients and mix well. Return to medium-low heat and simmer for about 15 minutes. Refrigerate in an airtight plastic container for up to 2 weeks.

SMOKED AND BRAISED PORK SHANKS

Pork shanks (or hocks) are basically from the bottom of the ham. They are lower down the leg, near the foot. This cut usually contains a lot of muscle and connective tissue and it is usually cooked for long durations to help break down that tissue. The end result, when cooked properly, is a beautifully tender and juicy piece of meat. In this recipe, I will be smoking the shanks first, and then braising them to perfection!

SERVES: 4 • COOK TIME: 4–5 HOURS

4 (16-oz [455-g]) pork shanks, bone-in

Salt and pepper

3–4 apple wood chunks

2 tbsp (30 ml) canola oil

1 yellow onion, diced

1 carrot, peeled and sliced

1 apple, peeled, cored and sliced

6 tbsp (90 ml) sherry vinegar

½ cup (120 ml) sparkling cider

1 sprig sage

2 qt (1.8 L) chicken stock

For this recipe, I will be using my insulated cabinet smoker and cooking at 325°F (163°C). If you are using an uninsulated bullet-style cooker (like a WSM), pay attention to the water pan and your fuel to make sure it doesn't run out of water or fuel and cook on the top cooking grate.

Season the shanks all over with salt and pepper.

Add the apple wood to the smoker, place the pork shanks in the smoker, and cook for about 1½ hours.

As the pork shanks cook, add the canola oil to a Dutch oven and heat over medium-high heat. Add the onion and carrot and cook, stirring occasionally, until browned, 5–7 minutes. Add the apple and sauté until golden brown, 3–5 minutes. Add the sherry vinegar and sparkling cider and cook until reduced by half, about 10 minutes.

Remove the shanks from the smoker and transfer to the Dutch oven. Add the sage and chicken stock to the Dutch oven with the pork shanks. Transfer the Dutch oven to the smoker. Cover and cook until the meat is almost falling off the bone, 2–3 hours.

Remove the pot from the smoker, remove the shanks from the pot and strain the liquid. Return half of the liquid back to the pot with the shanks, and place the pot back in the smoker. Roast until the meat is cooked through and fork-tender, about 30 minutes.

As the meat finishes, make a pan sauce. In a medium pot, cook the remaining half of the liquid over medium-high heat until reduced by half, 15–20 minutes.

Remove the meat from the smoker. Serve the shanks immediately with a drizzle of the reduced sauce.

LASAGNA WITH SHREDDED PORK

When I was a kid, I remember my mother making us spaghetti and sauce, but instead of meatballs or sausage, she would serve it with shredded pork. The pork wasn't smoked; it was roasted in the oven with some very simple seasonings. To me, it didn't matter how the pork was cooked, because it was so delicious—of course it was: my mother made it with love! Here is my take on a dish inspired by a childhood memory. I take the traditional lasagna, add some smoked shredded pork and cook the whole thing in a smoker! They key to this dish is using simply seasoned shredded pork. You want that nice smoky pork flavor to come through with the tomato sauce and cheese. Sounds good, right?

SERVES: 6–8 • COOK TIME: 1–1½ HOURS

2 (16-oz [455-g]) containers whole-milk cottage cheese (or ricotta)

16 oz (455 g) shredded mozzarella cheese, divided

8 oz (225 g) shredded Parmesan cheese

2 tbsp (4 g) chopped fresh oregano, divided

2 (28-oz [784-g]) cans crushed tomatoes (I like Tuttorosso brand)

2 tbsp (4 g) chopped fresh basil

4 cloves garlic, finely diced

1 tsp (2 g) onion powder

1 tsp (2 g) red pepper flakes

Salt and pepper to taste

1 (9-oz [252-g]) box lasagna noodles, cooked according to package directions and cooled

3 lb (1.4 kg) Simple Pulled Pork (page 133)

For this recipe, I like to use my insulated cabinet smoker; however, I will not be putting any water in the water pan. I will be cooking this at 325°F (163°C) for 1–1½ hours. If you are using an uninsulated bullet-style cooker (like a WSM), pay attention to the water pan and your fuel to make sure it doesn't run out of water or fuel and cook on the top cooking grate.

In a bowl, combine the cottage cheese or ricotta, 8 ounces (225 g) of the mozzarella cheese, Parmesan cheese and 1 tablespoon (2 g) of the oregano and mix well. Cover and keep chilled until ready to use.

In a large saucepan, combine the 2 cans of crushed tomatoes, basil, remaining 1 tablespoon (2 g) oregano, garlic, onion powder, red pepper flakes and salt and pepper to taste. Cook over medium heat for 15 minutes.

To assemble the lasagna, take about ½ cup (120 ml) of sauce and cover the bottom of a half-size disposable aluminum pan, then lay 3 lasagna noodles on top of the sauce. Take one-third of the cheese mixture and spread onto noodles, then add 1 pound (455 g) of the shredded pork and top with 1 cup (240 ml) of the sauce. Repeat 2 more times, then add a top layer of noodles, another 1 cup (240 ml) of sauce, and the remaining 8 ounces (225 g) mozzarella cheese.

Once the cooker is up to temperature, put the lasagna on the third rack space from the top and check after 1 hour. You will know when it's done because the edges will start to bubble. Remove from the cooker when done and let rest for about 20 minutes. Cut into squares and serve with the remaining sauce.

PIG WINGS

Pig wings? What are pig wings? Pig wings are made from the shank—a single bone surrounded by lean, tender meat. They look very similar to a chicken wing, but with that awesome pork flavor. They can also be cooked the same way as a chicken wing: baked, fried, grilled or smoked. I am going to show you how to smoke these so that they come out absolutely perfect each and every time! Be sure to ask your butcher for fresh/frozen uncooked pig wings. Most places will have pig wings, but they are precooked. Those are good in a pinch, but the fresh/frozen ones are better.

SERVES: 20 • COOK TIME: 2–2½ HOURS

5 lb (2.3 kg) uncooked pig wings

1 cup (128 g) Barbecue Seasoning Rub (page 182)

3-4 chunks apple wood

Sauce, for serving

For this recipe, I like to use my insulated cabinet smoker. Fire up your cooker to 225°F–250°F (107°C–121°C). Add about ½ gallon (1.8 L) of hot water to the water pan. If your cooker doesn't have a water pan, simply fill up a disposable aluminum pan and place it in the bottom of the smoker. If you are using an uninsulated bullet-style cooker (like a WSM), pay attention to the water pan and your fuel to make sure it doesn't run out of water or fuel and cook on the top cooking grate.

Take the wings and place them on a sheet of heavy-duty foil. Apply a good amount of barbecue seasoning to both sides of the wings.

Place them in the cooker and add the apple wood. Depending on the size of your cooker, you may not be able to fit the wings on one rack; if not, it's okay to put an even amount on each rack you use. Cook for about 2 hours. Start checking them around the 1½-hour mark and pull them when they have that nice mahogany color. The internal temperature should be about 160°F (71°C). If you were not able to get the uncooked pig wings, not to worry. Adjust your total cook time to about 1 hour.

When the wings are done, remove them from the cooker and toss with any sauce you want, such as the Honey BBQ (page 173), Alabama White (page 177) or Buffalo (page 178). Those are only some of my favorites. However, you can't go wrong with any of the sauce recipes, they are all great!

BARBECUE PARFAIT

At festivals and fairs, I have seen these concoctions called barbecue sundaes. These sundaes are layers of pulled pork, barbecued beans and coleslaw. They look tantalizingly delicious, so I just had to try one . . . and the happy gene turned on. I created my own version that adds some mashed potatoes to the mix. This is great for tailgating, but it's so delicious your family might request it just about every weekend.

SERVES: 4 • PREP TIME: 15 MINUTES

2 lb (910 g) Simple Pulled Pork (page 133), hot

2 cups (480 ml) Smokin' Hoggz Barbecue Sauce or Honey BBQ Sauce (page 173)

2 cups (300 g) Red Bliss mashed potatoes

1 cup (120 g) grated cheddar cheese

2 cups (500 g) Pork-Loaded Barbecued Beans (page 132)

2 cups (180 g) coleslaw

Place ½ pound (225 g) of the pulled pork on the bottom of a 4-ounce (112-g) mason jar and drizzle with barbecue sauce. Add ½ cup (150 g) mashed potatoes and top with ¼ cup (30 g) cheddar cheese. Layer in ½ cup (125 g) of the barbecued beans and top with ½ cup (45 g) of coleslaw. Drizzle with more barbecue sauce. Repeat this process with 3 more mason jars. Dig in!

CHAPTER 6

GOING WHOLE HOG

The practice of cooking a whole hog goes back centuries. People have prepared the whole hog using a variety of methods—slow cooking in an open pit, using a spit-style rotisserie and roasting in an enclosed metal box are a just a handful of techniques frequently used.

In different parts of the world, the whole hog is the main dish for a variety of occasions. For example, in the Caribbean region, whole hog is frequently the main dish at Christmas Eve gatherings, while in China it can be found at grand openings of businesses. Whole-hog cooking has accompanied all sorts of special occasions, including weddings, family reunions, community events and just about any other celebration that comes to mind.

In the 1800s, political candidates in the United States would travel from town to town and deliver speeches to draw electoral support. In rural regions, these speeches were sometimes delivered from atop tree stumps, and became known as stump speeches. In the South, stump speeches were sometimes accompanied with barbecue, and no doubt the barbecue was sometimes prepared whole-hog style.

In my eyes, whole-hog cooking is about the overall experience, and it's a great way to make any party or celebration more memorable. Cooking a whole hog can certainly be a challenge, though, and is a sure way to test your skills as a pit master. Some muscles in the pig are leaner than others, and different parts of the animal contain varying amounts of fat, sinew and collagen. This means that some parts of the pig will finish cooking before other parts. Your challenge as the pit master is to somehow cook the entire animal so that all of it is edible at the same time. The easiest way to do this is to cook the animal at a low temperature for a long period of time, and then pull or shred the meat for your guests.

So, what do you think? Are you ready to provide your guests with an outdoor eating experience they won't soon forget?

WHOLE HOG

There are many ways to cook the whole hog: belly up and butterflied, on a rotisserie, back side up or running style. I don't think there is a wrong way; it's whatever way you want and feel comfortable with. I am going to show you the belly up and butterflied way. I like this way because you are able to get some nice bark on the hams and shoulders.

SERVES: ABOUT 75–100 • COOK TIME: APPROXIMATELY 11–13 HOURS

TOOLS TO TRIM THE HOG

Electric reciprocating saw

A clean hatchet and mallet for cutting the legs and head and for splitting the backbone

Sharp boning knife

1 whole hog

2 gallons (7.6 L) Whole-Hog First Injection (page 165), plus more as needed

Yellow mustard

2 recipes Whole-Hog Dry Rub (page 166)

Vegetable oil

3–5 chunks apple wood

3–5 chunks sugar maple wood

1 recipe Whole-Hog Second Injection (page 165)

1 recipe Whole-Hog Finishing Sauce (page 167)

The instructions I will be providing here are going to be for a pig weighing about 100 pounds (45 kg); this should yield about 50 pounds (22 kg) of cooked pork, enough to make about 100 pulled pork sandwiches. It should also take 11–13 hours to cook.

Here are some approximate cook times, by weight, for cooking a whole hog at 250°F (121°C):

- 75 lb (34 kg): 8–10 hours
- 100 lb (45 kg): 11–13 hours
- 125 lb (51 kg): 14–16 hours
- 150 lb (68 kg): 17–19 hours
- 175 lb (80 kg): 20–22 hours
- 200 lb (91 kg): 23–25 hours

For this recipe, I will be cooking on a whole-hog cooker, an insulated cabinet smoker. I will be using the water pan filled with hot water and will be cooking at 250°F (121°C) for the entire cook. If your cooker doesn't have a water pan, simply fill up a disposable aluminum pan and place it in the bottom of the smoker.

If you don't have a whole hog cooker you can rent one, usually from the place you buy your hog from, or they can recommend someone who rents them. Or you can build your own out of cinder blocks; there are websites that show step-by-step instructions on how to build your own whole-hog pit.

ORDER YOUR HOG

Order your hog from your local butcher. Depending on how many people you are cooking for, I recommend ordering a hog that weighs 100–125 pounds (45–51 kg). You will probably need to give your butcher at least one or two weeks' notice before picking up.

(continued)

Whole hog ready for trimming on ice.

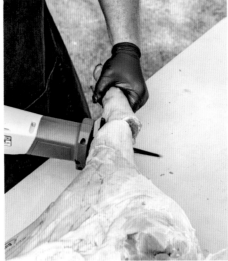
Removing lower part of the legs.

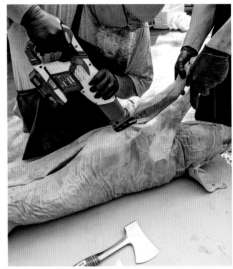
Cutting the breast bone.

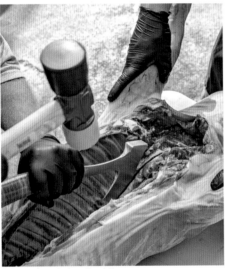
Splitting the spinal cord and ribs.

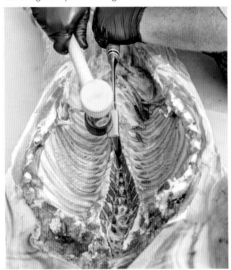
Splitting the spinal cord and ribs (continued).

Splitting the spinal cord and ribs (continued).

Peeling membrane from the ribs.

Removing excess fat from the ribs and belly.

Removing excess fat from ribs and belly (continued).

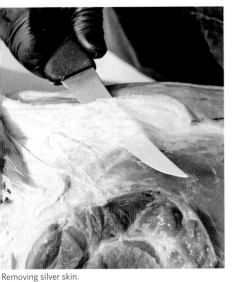
Removing silver skin.

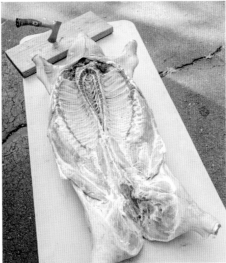
Final prepped hog ready for injection.

Injecting hams.

Injecting belly, ribs and loins.

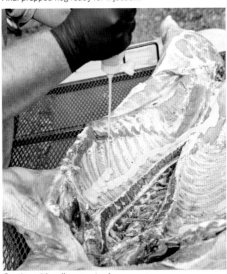
Coating with yellow mustard.

Applying rub.

Applying more rub.

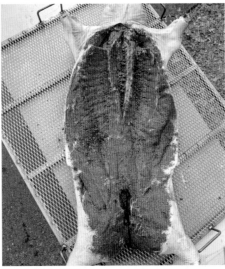
Hog ready for cooker.

Placing hog into cooker.

WHOLE HOG (CONTINUED)

TRIM YOUR HOG

I think trimming the hog is the most important step. It is during this step that you are able to remove anything that doesn't look good, and if I don't think it will taste good after it's cooked, it's going to get removed.

The first thing you want to do if the butcher hasn't done so is to cut the breastbone, which will allow you to spread the hog wide open to expose the meat on the inside. Then split the top of the spine just below the neck of the hog with an electric reciprocating saw. Now take a clean sharp hatchet and mallet, and starting from the top of the spine, cut until you get about three-fourths of the way through the length of the ribs. This will allow the shoulders of the hog to lie flat.

Next, with a sharp boning knife, remove as much fat from the top of the shoulders and hams as possible. Remove the membrane from the ribs and any extra silver skin you see on the meat. This will allow your rub and smoke to penetrate into the meat while cooking, and will also help create some real nice bark on the exposed meat.

Finally, remove all four feet at the joints with the reciprocating saw.

INJECT YOUR HOG

Inject the meat with at least 2 gallons (7.6 L) of the Whole-Hog First Injection (page 165). When injecting, place an emphasis on the meaty and fleshy parts of the animal, such as the hams, shoulders and loins. I recommend using a basic 2-ounce (60-ml) injector, which you can purchase at most supermarkets or department stores. As you squeeze the plunger to inject liquid into the meat, simultaneously withdraw the injector outward. This will help to more uniformly spread liquid throughout the meat. Don't worry about how many holes you create with the injection needle, just focus on getting as much liquid into the meat as you can. Puddling is likely to occur on the surface of the meat. Pat the puddles dry with paper towels.

If you are not cooking the hog right away, let it rest on ice now. When you're ready to cook the hog, remove it from the ice and pat the hog dry.

COAT YOUR HOG

Apply a coat of yellow mustard to the meat. The mustard will not season the meat. It creates a nice sticky layer so the rub will adhere. Do not let any mustard get on the exterior of the hog's skin or the skin will discolor during the cooking process.

Liberally apply Whole-Hog Dry Rub (page 166) on top of the mustard coating. Do not get any rub on the exterior skin.

Now clean off the skin of the hog. Using a cloth coated with vegetable oil, wipe down the skin. This will help remove any mustard or dry rub that stuck to the hog's skin, and will provide nice coloring during the cooking process.

START COOKING/SMOKING

Get your smoker ready to cook/smoke for about 13 hours (this also depends on the size of your hog; see the cooking chart on page 159). You're going to need a lot of charcoal, so I recommend using a good lump charcoal, such as Frontier brand. Place the hog on the smoker with the open cavity facing up. You want to cook at a constant temperature of 250°F (121°C). Once you place the hog into the cooker, add 6 to 10 chunks of smoke wood. I like to use a mix of apple and sugar maple.

(continued)

WHOLE HOG (CONTINUED)

WRAP YOUR HOG

About 6 hours into the cooking process, remove the hog and double wrap it in aluminum foil. This will help keep the hog from turning too dark and also traps all the juices inside so it will self-baste.

DO THE SECOND INJECTION

When the front shoulders reach a temperature of approximately 165°F (74°C), unwrap the foil, inject the shoulders, ham and loins with the Whole-Hog Second Injection (page 165), and rewrap.

Continue to cook the hog until the shoulders reach a temperature of 185°F–190°F (85°C–88°C) and the hams reach a temperature of 175°F–180°F (80°C–82°C).

APPLY THE FINISHING SAUCE TO YOUR HOG

Once the hog reaches the desired internal temperature, it's time to apply the sauce. Glaze the hog using the Whole-Hog Finishing Sauce (page 167). Cook the hog for another 30–45 minutes to let the sauce set.

At this point, the hog is ready to be served. Now, what I like to do here is stand behind the hog, carve out and serve my guests; this way, I get to explain to them the different parts of the hog they are eating. However, if you want to, you can shred the whole thing and make a pile of pulled pork and serve sandwiches. The choice is up to you. Have some fun and enjoy the fruits of your hard work!

WHOLE-HOG FIRST INJECTION

This is the injection I use for my whole hog, but you can use it for other parts of the pig like shoulders, butts, hams or ribs. This injection is a little on the sweet side, so it's a good balance with the natural saltiness of the pork.

MAKES: 3 QUARTS (2.8 L)

1 qt (940 ml) white grape juice

1 qt (940 ml) water

½ cup (144 g) kosher salt

½ cup (120 g) firmly packed brown sugar (light or dark)

½ cup (170 g) agave nectar or honey

½ cup (60 ml) apple cider vinegar

½ cup (64 g) Whole-Hog Dry Rub (page 166)

¼ cup (60 ml) Worcestershire sauce

¼ cup (60 ml) soy sauce

Combine all the ingredients in a large container and mix until the sugar and salt are dissolved.

WHOLE-HOG SECOND INJECTION

You want to use this injection when the meat of the shoulders and hams of the whole hog reach approximately 160°F (71°C). This will add another layer of flavor and help keep your meat nice and moist.

MAKES: ABOUT 2½ QUARTS (2.4 L)

2 qt (1.8 L) apple juice

1 cup (240 ml) apple cider vinegar

2 tbsp (16 g) Whole-Hog Dry Rub (page 166)

In a large container, combine all the ingredients and mix well. Store in the fridge until ready to use.

WHOLE-HOG DRY RUB

Not only is this a good rub for a whole hog, but you can also use this on just about anything, like beef and chicken. When using this recipe for a whole hog, you will want to make 2-4 batches, depending on the size of the pig, so you'll have enough.

MAKES: APPROXIMATELY 3½ CUPS (450 G)

1 cup (128 g) paprika

½ cup (64 g) mild chili powder

½ cup (120 g) firmly packed brown sugar (light or dark)

½ cup (100 g) sugar

¼ cup (32 g) coarsely ground black pepper

¼ cup (72 g) coarse kosher salt

2 tbsp (16 g) dry mustard powder

2 tbsp (12 g) onion powder

2 tbsp (12 g) granulated garlic

2 tbsp (16 g) ground cumin

2 tsp (6 g) cayenne pepper

Combine all the ingredients in a bowl and mix well. Store in an airtight container until ready to use.

WHOLE-HOG FINISHING SAUCE

This is what's going to make your whole hog really stand out. The sweetness of this sauce really helps balance out the overall flavor of the meat. This sauce isn't just for the whole hog; it can be used for anything you want. Go ahead and try it out!

MAKES: 1 GALLON (3.8 L)

2 qt (1.8 L) Smokin' Hoggz Barbecue Sauce or your favorite sauce

2 cups (480 ml) honey

1 cup (240 ml) white grape juice

1 cup (240 g) apricot jelly or jam

1 cup (240 ml) apple cider vinegar

In a large container, combine all the ingredients and mix well. Store in the fridge until ready to use.

CRACKLIN'S

Oh boy, are you in for a treat! Cracklin's are little pieces of pork fat with some of the skin still attached and deep-fried until crispy, then seasoned with salt. Here, I am going to mix things up a little and smoke them first, then hit them with high heat to make them nice and crispy.

SERVES: ABOUT 4 • COOK TIME: APPROXIMATELY 2–2½ HOURS

2 lb (910 g) pork skins with ¼–½" (6–13-mm) of fat on them

Kosher salt

¼ cup (32 g) Smokin' Hoggz All-Purpose Rub (page 181)

Cut the pork skins into 1-inch (2.5-cm) strips. You don't want to cut them into 1-inch (2.5-cm) squares yet, because they will fall through the cooking grates on your smoker! You can cut them up at the end of the cook.

Transfer the pork strips to a large stockpot and cover with water. On the stove top over medium-high heat, bring to a boil and cook for about 30 minutes. This step will render out some of the fat, but will keep just enough for what you need to make these delicious pork niblets.

After the skins come out of the boil, lay them out on a sheet pan skin side down and sprinkle with salt and the all-purpose rub. Don't discard the water after boiling the pork skins. Put it in the refrigerator and let it chill; any hard fat that develops on the top you can scrape off and use as lard, and the liquid left behind should turn gelatinous and you can use to add a richer flavor to soups and stews.

For this recipe, I like to use a non-insulated bullet-style cooker, and I will be cooking these at two different temperatures: low and slow at 250°F (121°C) for about 1 hour or so, then cranking it up to 425°F (218°C) for about another hour.

Fire up your smoker to 250°F (121°C), lay the pork strips on the top grate, skin side up, and cook for 1–1½ hours. Now crank up the cooker to 425°F (218°C) and cook for an additional hour, or until they are a nice golden brown.

When the pork skins are done, lay out some paper towels on a sheet pan and place the cooked pork skins on top to catch any extra grease. At this point, you can cut into 1-inch (2.5-cm) squares and reseason them with kosher salt and all-purpose rub. Let them sit for 10–15 minutes. When ready to eat, crack a cold beer and enjoy those *cracklin's!*

CHAPTER 7

SAUCES AND RUBS

This chapter contains several of the sauce and rub recipes that I use in this book. For the most part, these are original recipes I created for the book. Some of them are my take on the classic barbecue sauces and rubs I've learned about on the competition circuit. The Smokin' Hoggz Barbecue Sauce that I use at competition is a commercial product I have brought to market, and can be found online. If you are making a recipe in this book that calls for my Smokin' Hoggz Barbecue Sauce, and you don't have any on hand, feel free to swap it out with one of the sauce recipes in this chapter, such as the Honey Barbecue Sauce (page 173) recipe.

SIMPLE BARBECUE SAUCE

When you think of barbecue sauce, you're probably thinking of a sweet, tangy and thick sauce. That, in essence, is a Kansas City–style barbecue sauce. Because of the thickness of this sauce, it's not a really good marinade: it won't seep into the meat. Rather, this is a sauce you would use at the end of your cooking, to bring another layer of flavor to your meat! This sauce is great on just about any kind of meat, with baked beans and as a dipping sauce.

MAKES: APPROXIMATELY 3 CUPS (720 G) • COOK TIME: 40 MINUTES

2 tbsp (28 g) butter

1 small yellow onion, finely chopped

3 cloves garlic, minced

2 cups (480 g) ketchup

⅓ cup (110 g) molasses

⅓ cup (80 g) firmly packed dark brown sugar

⅓ cup (80 ml) apple cider vinegar

2 tbsp (22 g) yellow mustard

1 tbsp (8 g) chili powder

1 tsp (3 g) freshly ground black pepper

½ tsp cayenne pepper

Melt the butter in a medium saucepan over medium heat. Add the onion and cook until softened, about 5 minutes. Add the garlic and cook for another minute.

Add the ketchup, molasses, brown sugar, vinegar, mustard, chili powder, black pepper and cayenne pepper and stir to combine. Bring just to a boil and then reduce the heat to low and simmer until slightly thickened, about 30 minutes, stirring frequently.

Remove from the heat and let sit for about 30 minutes, then transfer the sauce to a blender or food processor and blend until smooth. Transfer to a jar and store in the refrigerator for up to a month.

HONEY BARBECUE SAUCE

Who doesn't love a good, sticky barbecue sauce that, after slathering some on those luscious ribs, makes you want to eat your fingers along with them? This sauce does just that. It's packed full of sticky honey goodness. Be careful and try to keep your fingers attached!

MAKES: APPROXIMATELY 2½ CUPS (600 ML) • COOK TIME: APPROXIMATELY 15 MINUTES

1 cup (340 g) honey

¼ cup (80 g) molasses

¼ cup (60 g) ketchup

¼ tsp ground cinnamon

½ tsp paprika

¼ tsp ground ginger

1 tbsp (18 g) seasoned salt

½ tsp ground black pepper

¼ tsp kosher salt

¼ tsp dried oregano

¼ tsp garlic

¼ cup (60 ml) steak sauce

2 tbsp (30 ml) Worcestershire sauce

1 tbsp (11 g) yellow mustard

1½ cups (360 g) firmly packed brown sugar (light or dark)

Combine all the ingredients in a medium saucepan and simmer for 15 minutes, until all the sugars are dissolved. Let cool, transfer to a jar and store in the fridge for up to 2 weeks.

BOURBON BARBECUE SAUCE

All barbecue cooks have their own special sauce with secret ingredients. Well, this one is no different. The bourbon in this sauce has a slight smoky, caramel flavor that pairs perfectly with pulled pork or pork ribs. There are a lot of good bourbons out there, so use your favorite. Yes, you can use Jack Daniel's Tennessee Whiskey—it's technically bourbon—but that's a story for another time!

MAKES: APPROXIMATELY 4 CUPS (910 ML) • COOK TIME: APPROXIMATELY 30 MINUTES

2 tbsp (28 g) unsalted butter

2 cloves garlic, minced

1 small yellow onion, minced

¼ cup (60 ml) bourbon

⅔ cup (160 g) chili sauce

⅓ cup (80 g) firmly packed brown sugar (light or dark)

1 tbsp (15 ml) Worcestershire sauce

1 tbsp (15 ml) apple cider vinegar

2 tsp (14 g) honey

2 tsp (6 g) dry mustard

2 tsp (6 g) chili powder

1 tsp (6 g) kosher salt

1 tsp (3 g) ground black pepper

½ tsp ground coriander

¼ tsp cayenne pepper

Heat the butter in a 4-quart (3.8-L) saucepan over medium-high heat. Add the garlic and onion; cook until soft, about 4 minutes. Stir in the bourbon, chili sauce, brown sugar, Worcestershire sauce, vinegar, honey, mustard, chili powder, salt, pepper, coriander and cayenne. Simmer, stirring, until thickened, about 30 minutes. Let cool, transfer to a jar and store in the fridge for up to 2 weeks.

CAROLINA GOLD BARBECUE SAUCE

The Carolinas are very unique in that there are regions within them that prefer one sauce style over another. Mustard sauce, brought by early German settlers, is very prevalent in South Carolina from Columbia to Charleston. It is usually made with yellow mustard as a base, but I am changing things up a little by starting with nicely pungent Dijon mustard. The next time you make some pulled pork—or any kind of pork, for that matter—you're going to want to put some of this sauce on it!

MAKES: APPROXIMATELY 4 CUPS (910 ML) • COOK TIME: 40 MINUTES

1½ cups (264 g) Dijon mustard

¼ cup (44 g) yellow mustard

½ cup (120 g) firmly packed brown sugar (light or dark)

¾ cup (240 g) honey

¾ cup (180 ml) apple cider vinegar

1 tbsp (8 g) chili powder

1 tsp (3 g) freshly ground black pepper

1 tsp (3 g) freshly ground white pepper

½ tsp cayenne pepper

1½ tsp (8 ml) Worcestershire sauce

2 tbsp (28 g) butter, at room temperature

1 tsp (5 ml) hot sauce

In a heavy, nonreactive saucepan, stir together the mustards, brown sugar, honey and vinegar. Add the chili powder and black, white and cayenne peppers. Bring to a simmer over medium-low heat, and cook for about 20 minutes. Do not boil, or you will burn the sugar. Mix in the Worcestershire sauce and butter. Simmer for another 15–20 minutes. Taste and season with hot sauce to your liking. Let cool, pour into an airtight jar and refrigerate overnight to allow the flavors to blend. The vinegar taste may be a little strong until the sauce completely cools. Store in the fridge for up to 2 weeks.

EASTERN CAROLINA VINEGAR SAUCE

Here is another sauce from the Carolinas. This one is heavily used along the coast of North Carolina. I like to eat my pulled pork with a little bit of vinegar sauce over the top of my sandwich. I love the bite of the vinegar and subtle heat from the red pepper flakes. This will be a thin sauce that lightly coats the pork and gets soaked up into the bun.

MAKES: 2¾ CUPS (660 ML)

2 cups (480 ml) apple cider vinegar

½ cup (120 g) ketchup

2 tbsp (30 g) brown sugar (light or dark)

2 tsp (12 g) salt

1 tbsp (5 g) red pepper flakes

1 tsp (3 g) cayenne pepper

1 tsp (3 g) ground black pepper

1 tbsp (15 ml) Worcestershire sauce

1–3 tsp (5–15 ml) hot sauce, such as Chipotle Tabasco

Combine all the ingredients in a bowl and mix until all blended. Transfer to a jar and store in the fridge for up to 4 weeks.

ALABAMA WHITE BARBECUE SAUCE

This traditional Alabama barbecue sauce uses mayonnaise as its base rather than tomato sauce, vinegar or any of the other traditional barbecue sauce bases. As with many barbecue sauces, you want to apply this only at the very end of your grilling or smoking. It will break down and separate if it is heated too long. You can use this sauce on chicken and turkey. It is also good on pork. Alabama white barbecue sauce has a tangy flavor that is a great addition to grilled or smoked foods. The first time I ever had this sauce was at my friend's wood-fired pizza restaurant. He told me, "You have to try it—it will blow your mind!" Here is my rendition.

MAKES: APPROXIMATELY 3½ CUPS (840 ML)

2 cups (480 g) mayonnaise

1 cup (240 ml) apple cider vinegar

¼ cup (80 g) agave nectar

1 tsp (3 g) garlic powder

2 tsp (6 g) chili powder

1 tbsp (8 g) coarsely ground black pepper

1 tbsp (18 g) salt

Mix all the ingredients in a bowl. Transfer to a jar and store in the fridge for up to 2 weeks.

BUFFALO SAUCE

I love Buffalo sauce! This sauce isn't just for chicken wings anymore: I put it on my eggs in the morning for breakfast, I use it on pork chops and I also use it on Pig Wings (page 152)!

MAKES: APPROXIMATELY 2 CUPS (480 ML) • COOK TIME: 10–15 MINUTES

2 tbsp (28 g) butter

1 cup (240 ml) hot sauce, such as Frank's RedHot

2 tbsp (30 ml) Sriracha

¼ cup (60 ml) Italian dressing

¼ cup (80 g) agave nectar

1 tbsp (8 g) chili powder

Salt and pepper

In a saucepan, melt the butter over medium heat, then stir in the hot sauce, Sriracha, Italian dressing, agave and chili powder and simmer for 5 minutes. Season with salt and pepper to taste. Let cool, transfer to a jar and store in the fridge for up to 2 weeks.

GARLIC BUTTER

Sometimes simple is better when you don't want the sauce to overpower the meat, just enhance its flavor. This is a great, simple sauce to apply at the end of the cooking process. I like to use it as a dip with bread and chicken wings or as a basting liquid for pork chops and Pig Wings (page 152).

MAKES: ½ CUP (112 G) • COOK TIME: 5 MINUTES

½ cup (112 g) unsalted butter

2 tbsp (12 g) chopped garlic

¼–½ tsp kosher salt

½ tsp black pepper

2 tbsp (4 g) chopped fresh parsley

In a saucepan over medium heat, melt the butter, then add the garlic, salt and pepper and cook for about 5 minutes. Remove from the heat, add the parsley and mix well. You want to use this sauce right away; if you let it sit too long the butter will harden.

TERIYAKI SAUCE

One night I was in the mood for some teriyaki sauce to have on my chicken wings. I had none in the house and really didn't feel like driving to the store, so I came up with a recipe and, surprisingly enough, I couldn't believe how good it was. I have since tweaked and fine-tuned my original recipe from that night. Here it is! This sauce is now a staple in my house.

MAKES: 1½ CUPS (355 ML) • COOK TIME: APPROXIMATELY 10–15 MINUTES

½ cup (120 ml) soy sauce

2 tbsp (30 ml) mirin

2 tbsp (30 ml) rice wine vinegar

1 tbsp (15 ml) sesame oil

¼ cup (60 g) firmly packed brown sugar (light or dark)

¼ cup (60 ml) pineapple juice

2 tbsp (12 g) grated ginger

4 cloves garlic, minced

2 green onions, diced

½ tsp black pepper

In a saucepan over medium heat, combine all the ingredients and simmer until the sugar is fully dissolved. Let cool, transfer to a jar and store in the fridge for up to 2 weeks.

SMOKIN' HOGGZ ALL-PURPOSE RUB

I put this recipe in the first book I wrote, and it is such a good rub recipe that I wanted to include it in this book too. This was one of the first rubs I developed a few years back, and I primarily used it on chicken, pork and seafood, and only during grilling events. Come to find out this rub is great on anything, including veggies! This is a very well-rounded rub with some great flavor, and will definitely bring a little pop to anything you cook.

MAKES: 3 CUPS (384 G)

¼ cup (32 g) ground chipotle powder

¼ cup (50 g) turbinado sugar

¼ cup (32 g) ground ancho chili powder

¼ cup (32 g) paprika

¼ cup (72 g) kosher salt

1 tbsp (8 g) ground cumin

1 tbsp (8 g) onion powder

1 tbsp (2 g) dried thyme

1 tsp (1 g) dried marjoram

1 tsp (3 g) cayenne pepper

2 tbsp (12 g) green peppercorns, crushed

1 tbsp (8 g) ground white pepper

1 tsp (2 g) celery seed or ½ tsp celery seed powder

½ tsp ground allspice

½ tsp ground cinnamon

½ tsp ground ginger

Mix all the ingredients in a bowl and store in an airtight container for up to 6 months.

NOTE: You can apply rubs anywhere from 1 hour before cooking the meat to mere moments before the meat hits the grill. As a general rule, you should try to apply a rub 1 hour before you cook.

BARBECUE SEASONING RUB

It's always a good thing to have some sort of basic barbecue seasoning on hand if you need to kick whatever food you're cooking up a notch. This barbecue seasoning is great on everything from homemade potato chips to veggies to any kind of meat. If you're going to use this on chips, sprinkle it on just after they come out of the fryer; for meat, apply just before you throw it on the grill.

½ cup (120 g) firmly packed brown sugar (light or dark)

½ cup (64 g) paprika

1 tbsp (8 g) ground black pepper

1 tbsp (18 g) salt

1 tbsp (8 g) chili powder

1 tbsp (6 g) garlic powder

1 tbsp (6 g) onion powder

1 tsp (3 g) cayenne pepper

Mix all the ingredients together in a bowl and store in an airtight container for up to 6 months.

JAMAICAN JERK SEASONING

Jerk is a style of cooking native to Jamaica in which meat is dry-rubbed or wet-marinated with a very hot spice mixture called Jamaican jerk spice. Jerk seasoning is traditionally applied to pork and chicken. Some of today's recipes also apply jerk spice mixes to all kinds of seafood, beef, sausage and lamb. Jerk seasoning principally relies on Scotch bonnet peppers. Other ingredients include ground cloves, cinnamon, green onions, nutmeg, thyme, garlic and salt. For this recipe, I substituted cayenne for the Scotch bonnet.

MAKES: 2 CUPS (256 G)

¼ cup (60 g) firmly packed brown sugar (light or dark)

1 tbsp (8 g) cayenne pepper

2 tbsp (36 g) kosher salt

2 tbsp (12 g) garlic powder

2 tbsp (12 g) onion powder

2 tbsp (4 g) dried thyme

1 tbsp (8 g) ground cumin

2 tsp (6 g) ground cinnamon

2 tsp (6 g) ground nutmeg

2 tsp (6 g) ground coriander

½ tsp ground ginger

½ tsp allspice

½ tsp ground cloves

Mix all the ingredients in a small bowl and store in an airtight container for up to 6 months.

ACKNOWLEDGMENTS

To my sister, Betsy, for graciously letting me use her house for an entire weekend to shoot the book.

My wife, Shaune Gillespie, for always giving me inspiration and keeping my head in the game.

My teammate and right-hand man (and sometimes left), Alan Burke, for always running block and doing the stuff I don't have the patience for.

Tim O'Keefe for helping me write this book, taking all my ideas and turning them into something that people can read and understand.

Ken Goodman for his incredible vision and always making the food look so amazing.

To my publisher, Will Kiester, my editor, Marissa Giambelluca, and the entire staff at Page Street Publishing for giving me the opportunity to do another book.

Eric and Cindy Mitchell for taking time out of their busy schedule to help with the photo shoot again.

Chad and Nicole Humphrey for spending two days prepping and cooking for the photo shoot, and for building the best smokers on the planet.

To all my barbecue friends, for being so freakin' awesome.

ABOUT THE AUTHORS

BILL GILLESPIE is the founder and head pit master for the World Champion Smokin' Hoggz BBQ team and author of *Secrets to Smoking*. Bill spends his days working for the local utility company as a design engineer, but his true passion is grilling and cooking barbecue. For more than 25 years, Bill has been perfecting his barbecue craft cooking in his backyard for friends and family. In 2005 Bill joined the barbecue circuit and in 2008 he formed Smokin' Hoggz BBQ. Since then, he has gone on to win multiple grand championships and numerous awards, including the Jack Daniel's World Championship Invitational Barbecue and the American Royal Invitational World Series of Barbecue—two of the most prestigious barbecue competitions on the circuit.

TIM O'KEEFE has a lifetime membership in the Kansas City Barbecue Society (KCBS), the largest organization in competition barbecue. Based out of the Boston area, his love of barbecue once inspired a cross-country road trip to Lockhart, Texas, just to eat brisket! Stops in Kansas City, Missouri; Gulfport, Mississippi; and Memphis, Tennessee; helped round out his understanding of regional variations in this unique American cuisine. A certified barbecue judge, Tim has judged over 30 contests sanctioned by KCBS. He has a master's degree in writing from Northeastern University, has contributed articles for *National Barbecue News* and co-wrote *Secrets to Smoking* with Bill Gillespie.

INDEX